STRACHAN STYLE

STRACHAN
STYLE
A LIFE IN FOOTBALL

GORDON STRACHAN
WITH KEN GALLACHER

MAINSTREAM
PUBLISHING

EDINBURGH AND LONDON

First published in Great Britain 1991 by
MAINSTREAM PUBLISHING COMPANY (EDINBURGH) LTD
7 Albany Street
Edinburgh EH1 3UG

ISBN 1 85158 403 X (cloth)

A catalogue record for this book is available from the British Libarary

Typeset in 11/13pt Garamond by Blackpool Typesetting Services Ltd
Printed in Great Britain by Butler & Tanner Ltd, Frome

*To my wife Lesley
and children Gavin, Gemma and Craig*

CONTENTS

BACK AT THE TOP

I HAVE A LOT TO THANK LEEDS UNITED FOR. THEIR faith in me restored my career at a time when I was sure I was simply going to be eking out my last few years as a player without making any further impact on the game as a whole. Instead, because of Howard Wilkinson's faith in me, I'm still playing in the First Division, still skipper of the team, and I've also captained my country THREE times after believing my Scotland days were over.

Oh, and there was also a little matter of winning the Player of the Year award from the English Football Writers Association. I was so happy to pick that up because I took it as an award for the team, as well as for me personally. It gave me hope that the efforts we have all made to give Leeds United a better image were working. If the Press decide to select you as their number one player for the season then you have to be doing some things right. And, if you are, then maybe there are a few more supporters out there learning to love Leeds. I hope so, because it has not just been about getting promotion and re-establishing the team in the First Division. It has also been about the image of the club. We want to be more popular. We want to rid ourselves of this handicap of being so disliked by so many fans of other clubs.

I doubt if all of that was justified, but whether it was or not doesn't matter today. What does matter is that we can present the club in a better way, play good football and impress on the world at large that this is a new Leeds United, a team which has put its troubled days in the past.

I have enjoyed these past seasons with Leeds – they have been like a welcome extension to an already full career. I don't know how long I will be able to keep playing without dropping the standards of fitness and skill which I have set for myself. The manager believes I can still be playing when I'm forty – I hope he's right. That would be

Back in the Scotland team – though the new "long drawers" didn't meet with everyone's approval. I didn't mind. All I wanted was to be back in the side.

the biggest bonus of all. I can remember Bobby Charlton saying to me at Old Trafford one day, not to give up too early. A lot of players have given up when they might have had a few more happy years in the game, and they have regretted it. I have no intention of being one of them. I'll play as long as I can and as long as I am enjoying the football. That counts for a lot, too. If it ever became a drudge to go into training or to get myself geared up for games then I think I would know it was time to quit.

So far that is not the case. There is a good feeling about Elland Road and I reckon I am savouring every moment of it more than I ever did before. When I was at Aberdeen and we were winning all those trophies, it was the start of a big adventure. Then one day, I looked around and decided that I had to move on. I wondered what had happened to the starry-eyed idealism I had when the trophies first began to arrive.

When I was at Old Trafford I knew that we were expected to win some trophy or another, and we did – in my first season. Then I found out that it wasn't enough. It was the FA Cup and it had its special prestige but it was not the First Division Championship. At Manchester United anything less than that is looked on as just OK – only a stepping stone to the REAL thing. Too many good people, players and managers have been sacrificed because of that title jinx and so while I had good times – especially with Big Ron – it was also an anti-climax after the first season and a half.

Leeds has not been like that at all. Leeds has been a club where everything has come right and where everything you do is appreci-ated – by the manager, the fans and the Board. After we had had that opening season in the First Division I knew that my contract had to be renewed and, no matter that I knew I had been a regular and that I had done well through the whole season, I still felt nervous. The age business haunted me again. I wondered if the Boss would want to keep me on for another two years. I shouldn't have worried. When the time came, he told me to go in and see Bill Fotherby and fix another two years. It's that kind of faith, that simple expression of trust which has done so much to keep me playing at a time when I thought it might all be over. And the players, too, the younger lads who are tasting some kind of success for the first time, others with a little bit more experience but still chasing honours and not being blasé about it all – they all help.

I'm that little bit older now. More mature. So I find myself sitting back at times and just enjoying the whole glorious thing that has happened to me, and is continuing to happen. Winning that Second Division title meant more to me than anything else I've ever won – because I am repaying a club and a manager for believing in me. It meant an awful lot because it had seemed to be a target which was going to be out of reach and then, amazingly, it was over. We had won, and we were back in the First Division where Leeds United should always be.

It was important to be there as the new Premier set up was being worked out. We achieved that and then, towards the end of October 1991, there was another milestone when we went top of the First Division table, the first time the club had held that position since their great days under Don Revie. It was something like seventeen years earlier that we last sat at the top of English soccer and it was a nice feeling.

Obviously we want more of that. The manager bought new players in the summer, he is changing the style of the team a little bit, and he knows that the better the quality of player he brings in then the higher the standard we will be able to reach. I would love to help Leeds win some kind of honour, love to get into Europe with them,

Home is where the heart is. Mine is here at Elland Road. This club, this set-up, revitalised my career.

love to see the club go on and on from what we have already been able to build.

I miss the European involvement – only the games with Scotland kept in touch with the game on the Continent – and it would be good to have a little final, farewell flourish in one of the tournaments. Playing for my national side against Switzerland and Romania in the European Championship matches brought back my appetite for that kind of game. I'm sure that we could be successful if we get the chance, because the Europeans don't relish facing up to our type of football. They don't have the same aggression, the same pace, the same directness that we have. I can hardly wait to get back and introduce some of the Elland Road lads to that level of football. It's coming for them and I just want to hang around a little bit longer until it does.

Leeds – and Life after Thirty

IT'S AN UNFORTUNATE FACT THAT IN THIS COUNTRY players are tossed aside when they reach the age of thirty. One day, you're doing fine and then, the next, you are a veteran or even a has-been. It's happened to so many players and it's totally unfair. It is not something that the continentals are guilty of doing to their experienced players. Their footballers are judged on the ability they possess, not on the birthdate they have. That's the way it should be and maybe the experience I have had with Leeds United will help to make the point for others who are about to cross that landmark age.

When the chance of a move from Manchester arrived I was undergoing another crisis of faith – wondering if I would be able to move on elsewhere and do a job for another club. I had lost faith in my own ability again, something that has plagued me down through the years. I knew that the manager, Alex Ferguson, had lost faith in me and I was not enjoying playing for the club in my last few months there. It seemed that Alex had given up on me. He thought that I had nothing left to give and that I was not going to be able to help him get the kind of success he wanted at Old Trafford. Maybe he was right. Certainly the position he was playing me in – wide on the right – did not suit me particularly. He felt he could get better players to go into that area and I suppose I agreed with that assessment.

One player he wanted was Trevor Steven, but he failed to get him when the English international decided to join Graeme Souness at Rangers. I also thought that he might go for David Rocastle of Arsenal. Both of them would have been valuable players for United and I admit that in the area he wanted to use them they would have been more effective than me. He had a certain style of playing and I was not exactly happy about the role I was handed.

I had always felt that there would be a question mark over my future when Ron Atkinson was sacked and Alex came in to take over. I was happy that he had got the job he wanted. He had told me after the World Cup in Mexico that it was the job he wanted most – one of two jobs which would tempt him away from Aberdeen, the other being Barcelona. He had turned down moves from Rangers, Arsenal and Spurs and it was the right time for him to make the break. But I just had this feeling that it would not work again for the two of us. We would be going over old ground and while it went all right for a while and I tried as hard as I could, I knew too much about his style of management and he knew too much about me. So with both of us

". . . I just had this feeling that it would not work again for the two of us."
Fergie and I share a joke. (Picture: *Daily Record*)

16

that bit older, it was never going to be a situation where the glory days of Pittodrie would be resurrected.

I guess we both knew that and while I played away for him in the first team I knew that a move was inevitable. At the end of that season my contract was up and I had a chance to move to the continent again and play for Lens in France. That turned into a bit of a farce. I went over there to find that they were in the middle of sacking their coach while they were also trying to sign me. Nothing seemed right. If I had gone it would have been just for the money and that was not a road I wanted to go down. I felt I had a lot to offer still and that would have been a bad move. The kids were crying, too, because I was leaving Old Trafford. So I signed for one more year – knowing that in Alex's eyes I was a stopgap.

He wanted someone else and I knew that. I also knew that when the new man arrived that was it – I was OUT. I didn't really relish waiting around until that happened so that year I drifted in a kind of no man's land, recognising that my time was just about up at Old Trafford but without any clear idea of where I might be able to continue playing at the level I wanted to remain at.

The chance of a move did come towards the end of the season, in March, and suddenly I realised that there could be life after Old Trafford. It had worried me that so many players who leave United tend to be caught in a downward spiral. It's as if you have been with the best, the élite, and after that nothing can ever be the same. It depressed me that this just might happen to me too. I didn't want that. I didn't want to be caught that way. I was thirty-two years old but I felt fit enough. I knew that I had plenty left in me – plenty of 'engine' or whatever you want to call it. The only problem I had was a loss of confidence in my own ability because the manager no longer believed in me. I knew that, or, at least, I felt that, and it affected me. Psychologically it was hard for me to handle. It was worrying. Now I found that confidence seeping back because I found three managers who believed enough in me to offer me another start.

Bruce Rioch came on from Middlesbrough and while I appreciated that and I felt pleased that he had considered me I didn't get down to talking business. I told him straight off that I did not fancy moving there. I just didn't think it was the club for me.

There was some talk of Queens Park Rangers coming in but that did not happen. What did materialise, however, was an offer from my old Manchester United boss Ron Atkinson to join him at Sheffield

My first meeting with Ron Atkinson – he was a great manager for me and he has become as great a friend

Wednesday. I had always had a tremendous relationship with Ron and he was desperate to take me to Hillsborough. In fact, at one stage he suggested that I come in as player-manager and he would move into a general manager's role. That was the way the talking went.

It reminded me so much of the good times at Old Trafford, but the playing and coaching, which was a major offer from him, did not appeal to me. I knew that others had done it. My former Scotland international team-mates, Graeme Souness and Kenny Dalglish, both did it at Ibrox and at Anfield but they did it with top teams. Here was I contemplating stepping down a Division and I felt I would have enough to do just concentrating on the playing side. To take on fresh duties as a coach or even as team manager would have been too much for me. It was hard to turn Ron down after all he had done for me in the past and all that he seemed ready to do for me at this critical stage of my footballing life. I realised, too, that while I did not feel I should take on the extra burdens of coaching while still a player, it was something which would have guaranteed my future for a quite a spell. That part was tempting. Also, it had its appeal because I do fancy the idea of staying on in the game as a manager or even as a coach. But this just did not seem the right time to do that.

Again, by this time I had met Howard Wilkinson and I had been impressed by all that he said to me. Until that meeting I would have said that it was a foregone conclusion that I would be teaming up with Big Ron again. But when I eventually went down to see Ron things had changed. The men from Elland Road – Howard Wilkinson and the general manager Bill Fotherby – had more or less convinced me. I knew Ron was serious that day when he offered me his last biscuit – if you have ever seen Ron eat then you would know that was his final offer. But I told him the coaching side would be too difficult to do while I was also trying to establish myself as a player in a new setting.

It was all going to be hard enough, as it was. I realised that people would be looking at me and re-assessing me in my new surroundings. All the old chestnuts would inevitably be trotted out. I was over thirty, so a lot of fans would have me over the hill. It's funny but if you are under thirty and you have a bad game then that's it – you're rotten, just plain and simple bad. But if you are over thirty then your legs have gone. You're finished. I knew that I would have bad days as well as good ones and I knew I would have to handle that type of criticism and not allow it to get me down.

Above all, though, Howard Wilkinson had sold me Leeds United and the vision he had of the club's future. Leeds had been one of the really big clubs in England but had fallen on hard times. He was out to change all of that and he was able to get the message across to me that he WOULD change it. I left the meeting with the Leeds' people feeling excited at the prospects they had laid in front of me.

Remember, I was an experienced player who had been around a bit. I had been at three clubs, known success at two of them and played in two World Cups with Scotland. What I'm trying to say is that I was far from being a starry-eyed youngster, a teenager coming into the game who was ready to be impressed by the first manager he met. Here I was, a cynical old pro, and I was convinced that Leeds were going to go places. I'm happy now to point out that I was right in my judgment this time.

I had always had a kind of romantic notion that when I left Old Trafford it might be nice to go to a club which had been a major force at one time but had then known hard times, and to try to help them back to the top. I had thought about Aston Villa and Newcastle

An unorthodox tackle to say the least. Ronnie Whelan is my victim as Bruce Grobelaar looks on in this game for Manchester United against Liverpool

United in these terms but here were Leeds United making me an offer. They had a manager who believed in me and who believed that I could do the kind of rescue job I wanted to do. It just seemed right for me, for Howard Wilkinson, for Leeds United. My one worry was that it seemed just too perfect – but I decided to go ahead and it has been a move I have never once regretted.

I was so sure of the future, so sold on the club and its ambitions that I moved house to the Leeds area as soon as I possibly could. I believe that if you are playing for any club then you should stay close to where the team plays and where their fans live. That way you become a part of the community. You are right there among the supporters and close to the other players at the club. I didn't want people seeing me coming through from Manchester every day as if I was signing for the club just to make a few quid as I played out my last remaining seasons. I had a horror of people thinking of me as a kind of mercenary. Sure, the money was good but I felt that I wanted to earn every penny the club were paying me. To do that properly I wanted to be a part of the local scene. That's what I aimed to do at the outset and it's what I have tried to do ever since.

Throughout my life I have been like that with everything I do. If I go into something then I have to go into it all the way. There is no way that I want to be half-hearted once I have committed myself to any course of action. I genuinely believe that is the one way to do things.

In any case the club were committing themselves to me and that was important. I had been having nagging fears over my own ability because of the way things had been going at Old Trafford. Now I had met a manager who had faith in me and I knew that I had to repay that. He had confidence in me – and that, in turn, brought my own confidence back again. He told me that he would be depending on me a great deal as he set about launching the new Leeds United. I was his first major signing though he has made a few since my arrival. It was, I suppose, something of a gamble for him and I just wanted to make sure that it was the start of something big for him and for the club. And a bright new beginning for myself . . .

Dropping into the Second Division was an obvious worry for me. Ask anyone in England and they will tell you the same story – it is not an easy League to play in. And it's a very hard League to get out of. You have to be really good to get promotion because there are a lot of good teams there and a lot of good players. It is very, very competitive. I knew all of that before making my move but there are times when you dismiss all the knowledge you think you have and act on instinct. There are times when you just have a gut feeling about something – I had that about signing for Leeds United.

There are times when you meet someone and straight away you recognise that he is a crook, or, at least someone who is not to be trusted. And then there are other times when you meet someone and you just know that this is a man you can trust. It was one of these occasions for me when I met Howard Wilkinson.

When he took over as manager of the club they were down at the bottom of the Second Division and in deep, deep trouble. When he bought me they were eleventh or twelfth in the table with the remotest outside chance of getting into the promotion play-offs. There was never really a chance that we would make it, though the fans hoped against hope that it might just happen. I knew, therefore, when I signed, that there was still a way to go in his re-building plans.

Flying through the air, OK – but not with the greatest of ease. I'm heading for a muddy landing

When the deal had been finalised he told me that he hoped to win promotion the following season. That was the one thing he did not convince me about – but he was right.

When I first got to the club I looked around me and I thought that it would not happen the way he wanted it to happen. I could not see us being ready in a year to make the jump from the position we were in to the First Division. I just hoped that by the end of my two-year contract that we would be in that First Division and that I would have made a contribution to that achievement. That was what I expected and what I would happily have settled for. Shows how much I know – the next season we were champions and when my time scale was up we were sitting fourth from top of the First Division!

I don't think it is possible to over-estimate the work done by Howard Wilkinson since he took over at Elland Road. He told me that he had a lot of money to spend when I joined up and that has been the case. But the great thing is that he has made no mistakes at all in his deals as far as I can see. He does a lot of homework on his signings. I think he delves into the players' backgrounds before he makes any moves at all, because the characters he brings to the club are important to him. Leeds had had a bad image, partly because of trouble from some of the supporters and partly too because of some of the myths which grew up around the team Don Revie built in the late Sixties and early Seventies.

In the time I have spent under Howard at Leeds, he has been a tremendous influence. I have watched very carefully how he handles his big money transfers and I have listened to his views on the game and they were different from anything I had heard from any manager before. Yet they struck a chord with me. I knew this was sound soccer sense.

Maybe it was the transfer which opened my eyes to other aspects of the game and maybe it was just that I was willing to listen to him and ready to take on board any new ideas which would help me through the difficult settling-in period. It was a new challenge, after all, and I needed all the help and advice I could get.

Good players who have become managers or coaches seem to expect other players to be of the same standard as they were in their own playing days. It doesn't work that way. It's only now that I realise that there are different standards for different players, and that is just something you have to live with. You have to use the talents that players possess in the best way possible for them and for the team. You simply don't ask players to do something that is beyond their particular talents. That sounds simple enough, but it was not obvious to me until I made the move, watched Howard Wilkinson at work and listened to him as he outlined his philosophy on the game.

Basically he talks about winning football – about how you go about winning games. Without any doubt he has converted me. He has helped turn me into a more direct player without attempting to curtail me too much. I have not lost any of the flair I had before, or the little bits of individualism, but he has made me think more about other players and how to get the best out of them. He has taught me to examine how other players will react to situations on the field and

This is against Manchester City and I've just chipped the 'keeper. You'll have to take my word for it that I scored . . .

also to appreciate their limitations. Every player is not going to react the same way as I do, or the way that Bryan Robson or Norman Whiteside had done when I played alongside them at Old Trafford. A year or two back I could not understand why other players in the team were not always able to read me when I was in possession, or could not grasp what I was preparing to do with the ball. Now, because of his guidance, I have a better understanding of the players round about me, and a better feel for their problems on the field.

One of the myths about our gaffer is that his training is physically hard. It is not nearly as hard as I have known elsewhere and not a fraction as hard as outsiders like to believe. He does believe in long training sessions, and he also switches the timing of the sessions around so that you are not always working-out at the same time every day. That breaks any monotony that may set in, but I don't find these work-outs boring in any way. I have never minded one little bit that we often have extended sessions because I can see the benefits which arrive at the end of all the work.

A lot of the work is done on set pieces and that can involve a great deal of repetition. Corner kicks and free kicks, and even throw-ins, are practised and practised again and again until you get them off pat. He wants to have these absolutely right, because he knows how many goals can come from such situations. When a new player arrives at the club it's funny watching his reaction to the amount of work which is done, the detailed work which is so important to the success of set pieces when it comes to actual games.

You know, we could spend an hour to an hour and a quarter every Friday making sure that a set piece is going to be perfected. That pays off for us though, because we have a high success rate, a lot higher than with any other club I have played for. We worked out a lot of clever free kicks with Aberdeen and we got goals from them, but not to the extent these things have worked for us at Elland Road. The manager recognises that goals can come from set-piece situations and he wants to exploit them as much as he possibly can. We have won a fair number of important games from goals scored after corner kicks for example, and from free kicks too.

We have done magnificently with the set plays, but there is more to our game than that. Last season when I was with Scotland I was speaking to the Celtic assistant manager, Tommy Craig, and he said that he had seen us play a lot. He reckoned that we were the hardest working team in English football. He said that we all worked well for each other, and he had not seen any other team in the country do it as well as we did. I got a kick out of that and I could hardly wait to get back to Elland Road and tell the rest of the lads about it. It was a compliment and when you get that kind of praise coming from someone outside the club it means a lot. Actually there have been a lot of complimentary things said about us over the past year and that, I'm sure, has helped the image of the club.

People have not only commented on how we play the game, they have also talked or written about the HONESTY in our play. The manager will not tolerate anyone rolling round feigning injury, and if any player does do that then he can expect to land in trouble. And I mean serious trouble. The manager hates cheating of any kind and he just won't tolerate it from his own players. He has hammered that into all of us and we all feel the same way about it. As players we don't want anyone letting us or the club down by cheating.

We are all very conscious that the club has suffered from a bad image in the past. That doesn't annoy me – but I would be annoyed if I was Johnny Giles or Eddie Gray or Billy Bremner, because the team they were a part of played some wonderful football and yet too

Heading for another fall as I fail to evade this challenge . . .

often today they are described as if they were a team of thugs. They deserve to be remembered for the football they played and the trophies they won. Sadly, the hard man image has overshadowed all of the finer things from that era.

It was only after I had signed that I began to realise how unpopular Leeds were as a team. Opposing fans don't like us and we have had to learn to live with that. But it is unfair, especially when the gaffer and the lads have all been working so hard to change all of that. I think that we have had a better deal from the Press since we moved into the First Division and I think it helped too when I was named the Football Writers' Player of the Year. Maybe people are realising, at last, what the manager is trying to do at Elland Road. We want a better image for the club and we won't rest until we have succeeded in getting that. The club have already built a new family stand, and it's as good a family area as any in the country. It's all part of the new Leeds and that side is as important, at this time, as achieving success on the field.

I have thrived on the extra responsibility that Howard Wilkinson has given me since I signed for the club. He makes it plain what he wants me to do on and off the field as the club captain. But he doesn't have to spell it out all the time, as I have found that I'm on the same wavelength as he is. He looks for leadership by example and that's what I try to give him. He's not daft. He knows how I live my life and he wants me to pass some of the things I have learned on to the younger lads. If I see a young player stepping out of line, I'll have a word with him and hopefully he will listen to me and get back to the good habits he is being taught – the habits that will make him a real footballer. I try to make myself available to the young players, try to be on hand to give them advice when they need it. I suppose I take my captain's duties pretty seriously.

For instance, at the start of every season I give the new lads a little talk and tell them what is expected from them at the club. It's good fun. It's humorous and it's informal and I think that helps the lads relax a bit. They don't feel over-awed or scared as they might do if it was the manager laying down the law. This is me, just one of the players, and all I do is lay down guidelines for them to follow. I know they won't always be angels but I try to tell them when they should be drinking and when they should not. I warn them to stay away from the older players and get on with their own careers and while there is never any way you can live their lives for them you can give them some help. You can stop them falling into some of the traps you fell into yourself as a kid. You have been over it all before and you can see the pitfalls before they do and, hopefully, they listen and they learn. You can only hope that you get your message through to them. But if you try to set an example to them then that helps. That's how I handle it. I try to practise what I preach and I always encourage them to come to see me if they feel they have any problems which need to be sorted out. If they are in any kind of trouble, my reckoning is that they will always find it easier to talk the matter out with me or another senior professional, rather than with the manager. It can be a little bit intimidating to knock on the manager's door and stand there waiting for him to ask you to come in. You're talking here of a kid who is probably living away from home for the first time in a strange city, and really having no one to turn to for advice. Going to the Boss with some trouble you have landed yourself in can be scary. So I'm there and I make myself available whenever they want to talk things out. I think it has helped some of them. I hope so.

If they do have to see the manager, then the least I have been able to do is break the ice a bit for them, allowed them to get it off their chests and advised them how to handle things from there on in. The problems haven't been all that many because there is a good bunch of lads at the club. It reminds me of the camaraderie we had at Pittodrie. That says a lot for the manager's buying ability. He has shown that his judgment has been shrewd as he goes into the transfer market in his bid to restore the glories of the club.

You can be unlucky when you are following a policy of buying success – and yet there is no real alternative to that policy. Not in the situation Leeds United were in when Howard Wilkinson took over. He had to turn the place round quickly, because no one has time to wait for a youth policy reaching fruition. That is a luxury few managers are ever allowed. So managers are forced into the market place and sometimes when that happens things can go sadly wrong. You can get the kind of player who is only there for the money and is looking towards his next move, almost as soon as he comes through the front door. That's no use to any club.

You don't get that kind of soccer mercenary at Leeds, because our gaffer wouldn't have them. I reckon that because he goes so thoroughly into their off-field background there is very little chance of ever picking up a bad 'un. It hasn't happened by chance that we don't have any bad apples; that's come about because the manager vets the players so thoroughly. He wants to bring pride back to the club. Pride and prestige are his twin aims.

He stresses pride all the time – pride in what you do and pride in the club you play for. I think all of us at Leeds have that now. Certainly that is what I wanted when I left Old Trafford. I wanted the chance to put something back into the game, channelling my experience back to help the younger lads coming after me, and then

My international days are back again.
(Picture: *Daily Record*)

being able to see something growing again. That has been happening at Elland Road over the past two years, and we just want to keep it going.

I have another contract, one which has me tied to the club until I am thirty-six, and the gaffer believes that I can play until I'm forty. We'll see, but one thing is sure and that's the fact that this was the right move for me. I was lucky to get this chance, lucky to come to a club where people believed in me again and lucky to arrive when everything was taking off. The worries I had of disappearing from view when I left Manchester have vanished. This has been like a whole new career for me, and even my Scotland connection has returned. So much so that I was even captaining my country in some of the European Championship games.

That was something I thought had gone for good. Leeds and Howard Wilkinson helped bring my international days back. I owe them for that and I just hope I can repay them for all they have done for me.

The Start of Something Big

WHEN THE FIRST FULL SEASON WITH LEEDS KICKED off the manager had appointed me club captain. He said at the time that he felt I would be able to cope with the pressures which would undoubtedly build up over the season. As far as I was concerned I was convinced that there would be some difficult times ahead. Although the Boss had spent a lot of money and the Chairman, Leslie Silver, had made that cash available I still wondered if we would be good enough to claw our way out of the Second Division. The club had been attempting a First Division comeback since being relegated in 1982. The road back was a hard one, with lots of difficult opposition and hard places to travel to. When the fixtures were announced for the new season we found that out straight away. I knew I would not have too long to wait until the hard times started to close in around us.

Coping with the pressures came early. Too early for me, as I began to wonder what had hit us. That opening game was at Newcastle, a side relegated the previous season and as determined as ourselves to get back to the top flight. They are an ambitious club and, like ourselves, a club with a magnificent pedigree despite having fallen on hard times. It was as tough a beginning as we could have expected. We travelled north to St James's Park – and then returned empty handed after receiving a thorough beating. Mick Quinn, their striker, scored four of the goals as we slumped to a 5-2 hammering. We were without Chris Fairclough and also new signing Vinny Jones, but there was a warning for us in that result and we knew that we had to face another newly relegated club in our second match. At least, I thought, that one is at Elland Road.

Middlesbrough, with former Scotland captain Bruce Rioch in charge, were going to be no pushovers. Yet we also knew that this was a match where we had to get a victory. If we failed to do that then we would be liable to drop way behind our rivals. By the end of the season we expected both Newcastle and Middlesbrough to be among those who were challenging at the top. It was not going to be easy – in fact, I was wondering if there were to be any easy games in this cut-throat League. I was soon to find the answer. It was a resounding 'NO'.

Still, we did win against Middlesbrough, even though it took an own goal to give us the final edge in a match which confirmed all that I had been warned of about the Second Division. It is not an easy place to play, and it is certainly not an easy place to win promotion from. Our next couple of matches simply underlined that. We failed to beat Blackburn Rovers at our own place, and then slipped up against Stoke at their Victoria ground for another draw. Then we had to meet Ipswich. Again it was in front of our own support but again we let them down. We went in front but lost an equaliser and after our opening five games we had just half a dozen points, we were twelfth in the League and the fans were beginning to get a little fed up. So were we. Then we started to turn the corner and two wins in succession lifted us up the League and gave our spirits a boost at the same time. I managed to get a hat-trick in that match against Swindon after opening my scoring for the season against Stoke with a penalty kick. There was another penalty against Swindon and I also

Leeds boss Howard Wilkinson, the man whose faith in me kicked off a whole new career

scored with a header – something really unusual for me. John Hendrie hit the bar with a shot and it bounced out to me. I sent in a header which finished in the net. We had beaten Hull 1-0 the week before and now we felt that we were on our way, just three points off the lead and beginning to look like the team the Manager wanted us to be.

The great thing about those early days was the way the manager and the coaching staff behaved. They had a belief in what they were doing at the club. They had bought the players, and they were sure that they had bought the right players. Given that we were to use the good habits they were drilling into us at training every day then they knew that it would all turn out right in the end.

Their attitude helped carry us through because that was a rocky start. When you begin that way it is often very, very hard to make up lost ground. Sometimes it can be impossible. A side gets a bad start, becomes bogged down, and before you know it they are left behind in any title race. The character we had in our side saw us refuse to buckle after that poor opening and once we began to string together the performances the manager wanted, the results began to follow. We moved steadily up the table and while we always knew that it would be a tight finish to the season we had refused to panic, refused to alter our basic way of playing and stuck to the manager's deep-held playing principles.

It's happened in the past that teams have suddenly altered their style in a bid to change their run of results and it has had the opposite effect. Teams who do that generally go under. Our Boss took a little bit of stick, some harsh criticism from the terracings, especially after the disappointment of the home draw with Ipswich, but he had the strength to persist with his own ideas and with the players he had brought to the club. Howard Wilkinson, I always felt, knew what was needed to get a club OUT of the Second Division. That was not necessarily the same as what would be needed to stay in the First Division, once you got there. Hence the changes which followed our promotion success and the further changes after we had managed to stay in the top League. But I'm running ahead of myself here . . . we had a campaign to get through and we had the right man leading us.

There were other hard times ahead but that was always what we had been expecting and all that mattered at the end of the season was that we would finish up on top. Gradually, as the season wore on, so our own self-belief grew. I think if I could compare it with anything it was a little like the Aberdeen assault on Europe when we won the Cup Winners Cup in Gothenburg. As round followed round in that season, there was a feeling that we were going to win it. Even when we found ourselves against the legendary Real Madrid in that final in Gothenburg we didn't consider defeat.

It was a little like that, although obviously it was a more drawn out affair as title races always are. Championships are the true measure of consistency. They test you more than any Cup run can do. I can still remember now how exhausted I felt when that season ended. I have never been so drained, so utterly tired. I was glad that I had not been chosen for the World Cup Finals in Italy, because I did not think I would be able to look at another football for six months or so.

We began to grind out the results that the club needed, and the battle for the title broke down into an all-Yorkshire affair between ourselves and Sheffield United. We sat on their heels for a time, then we were joint top and then we went ahead. It was not good for our nerves . . .

A revenge win against our other promotion rivals, Newcastle United, helped us to the top. Ian Baird scored with a header to help ease the memory of that opening day defeat at St James's Park. Soon after that, though, Ian went out of the side. The Boss bought Lee Chapman for £400,000, and he was to become our main striker for the remainder of the season. Injuries began to bite but the Boss was helped by the Board. Mr Silver, a great man for Leeds, unloosened the purse strings. Again!

Chris Kamara and Imre Varadi both appeared and came into the team as the run towards the First Division continued. There were some amazing games, some when it looked as if we were to blow it, others when we dominated. I can remember a Yorkshire derby with Hull, who were fighting relegation. We were down 3-2 in the second half – the first time we had lost as many goals at home. I scored the winner that day but the goal of the season was the opener from Vinny Jones, a spectacular shot which had given us the lead and should have pushed us beyond Hull's reach. But in those nervy days anything looked possible, even a shock win by Hull. It didn't happen and we held on to our challenging position.

By now we had been handed another target by the Boss. He wanted ninety-two points from us to make sure of the title and the promotion we so desperately wanted. It was a tough task and a hard target, but the manager was clearly telling us that we had to keep

It is hard getting away from defenders in English football. See for yourselves!

winning, keep getting the results, keep battling to stay ahead of our rivals.

Then we hit a bad spell, one which came close to wrecking all our dreams. Unbelievably, we went on a run of games which added pressure unlike any I'd ever known. We could not get the wins we required and after being ten points ahead of Sheffield United with only nine games left, we were hauled back to level top, staying just in front because of a better goal difference. But there was danger lurking in third place now as well because a Newcastle revival had carried them back into the frame.

It was now we knew we were to be tested. There had been an obsession at the club about going up. It was the first time that I had known anything so intense in football. We had been told that the First Division was our goal. It was what the club wanted. What the club needed. We had to achieve that aim. We had to achieve it for the Chairman, who had sunk so much money into financing this dream. We had to do it for the Manager who had brought so many of us to Elland Road to make certain that promotion would be won. And then too there were the fans, who had waited so long and for the most part so patiently, for a return to the First Division. The tension inside the club when we began to lose ground was indescribable. It affected us all. Even those of us who had been over similar courses in the past were caught up in it all.

I still look back with embarrassment at my own behaviour when we played Bradford at Elland Road. I just flipped at the end of the game. We were winning 1-0 and it had been difficult, even though Bradford had the worst away record in the League when they arrived at our place. But we thought we had done it. Then, late in the game, I had chased a ball deep into their half and taken my time coming back out when the goalkeeper cleared upfield. I had not galloped back to stay onside because with just a minute to go there seemed little point in that as we were a goal in front. When one of our lads booted it back into their half I was caught – but it was not something which concerned me. We tended to do that at Leeds, take our time when it suited us and make sure the free kick would be taken as far from our goal as possible. This time, though, the referee, a Mr John Martin, decided to allow the Bradford lads to take the kick twenty yards ahead of my position, almost on the halfway line. While I protested it made no difference to him. His mind was made up and the ball went soaring downfield into our penalty box. Peter Haddock made a tackle, one of their lads took a fall and they were given a penalty. They scored to make it a perfect finish for me. We had lost two very valuable points. It was unbelievable and I quite simply lost my temper.

It was out of character for me, but I went nuts. Right over the top. I had a go at the referee in the tunnel, though I can't remember too much about that. My wife, Lesley, saw that part of it and told me later she had never seen me behave like that before. Hopefully she'll never see me like that again. I barged into the dressing-room, kicking the tables and the benches and shouting and bawling at the other

*A little bit of temperament here after I had a goal disallowed against Brighton.
Off came my jersey but it's going back on and I'm able to laugh at myself.
We must still have been winning*

players. The manager was looking at me and wondering what the hell was going on. I had just gone and I think people were scared to touch me in case I simply exploded, went up in a puff of blue smoke. Then Jim Beglin stood up and said, "Sit down and shut up." I had a go at him then and he threatened, "Shut up or I'll whack you in the jaw. You're out of order." That quietened me down. I collapsed on to the bench.

I felt rotten after that outburst because it was out of character. The Boss had made me captain and he wanted me to set an example and here I was going mad about a decision. My only explanation afterwards – and I have thought a lot about it since – is that the tension we were all under simply boiled over for those five minutes or so. I needed a release, a safety valve, and that was it. But I wish I hadn't done it because if more people had seen me in that tunnel then the image we had been carefully nurturing all the way through the season would have been damaged. I knew that I was out of order and I knew, too, that we had to come back and that I would have to help make amends. I got the chance when we played our closest rivals, Sheffield United, at Elland Road.

This was a crunch game – weren't they all at that stage? – a local derby, against the team who had been duelling with us for the number one spot in that Second Division since early in the season. We had to win. By now the Boss had set another target for us – four wins from our last six games he wanted and he was convinced that would be good enough to take the title.

On that day against Sheffield we were at our very best. This was the way the Boss had wanted us to play. We were positive and power-ful. Entertaining and effective. And we won well by four goals to nil as Sheffield showed their own signs of wear and tear from the title battle. I scored twice, which helped make amends for the Bradford bust-up. I grabbed the first and then after Lee Chapman scored – his goals were now so important to us on the run-in – I scored another with a penalty. Colin Speed finished it off. That's that, I thought, that's promotion. All we have to do is keep playing like that and no one can stop us. The following week we went to Brighton and we drew 2-2 and worse was yet to come . . .

The next match was another Yorkshire derby, against Barnsley, who were struggling to stay in the Second Division. They beat us 2-1, gave us our first home defeat of the season, and clinched their own survival. It did nothing for us and we knew we were running out of

Getting a winner in a vital promotion battle against Hull City. It helped us into the First Division

games as the season wore remorselessly on. All the games were crucial, with Sheffield United and ourselves still together at the top and Newcastle only two points away.

In our last home game we played Leicester City, and the fans forgot their own frayed nerves to turn out and support us. They inspired us to a victory. Ironically this win was almost snatched away from us by the Leicester midfield man Gary McAllister – who was to join us for a million pounds in the summer. Maybe it was his performance that day which convinced our gaffer to spend all that money on him. He's a good mate now, at the club and with Scotland, but I could have seen him far enough that day. We had been winning through a first-half goal from Mel Sterland, another notable buy for the club from Rangers. Then after we had missed chances Gary stepped in to equalise and soon after that he almost scored a second. Only a wonderful save from Mervyn Day stopped him. Before the end came I scored with a shot from the edge of the box and if you look at the television pictures of the players lifting me up on the

Down but not out. This is me after getting that winner against Hull

touchline you will see one very tired man. I look almost skeletal – and I think I was feeling even worse than I looked!

It didn't help when the wrong score was flashed from Newcastle and the fans outside thought it was all over. Some of the players did too – Vinny was up in the stand taking a bow. But they'd got it wrong. We had another game to go, another win to notch before this long, long season was over.

We went to Bournemouth on Bank Holiday weekend and we won. Lee Chapman scored and it was over. The only sour note was some trouble from the supporters who, until then, had been magnificent. It spoiled the party a little – but nothing could really spoil it. The title meant too much to all of us for even crowd trouble to dampen our spirits. Mainly, though, I experienced a deep-down sense of relief that it was all over, that we had done it at last, that we had reached the goal set for us. We did not reach the ninety-two points the manager had asked for – we were seven short of that – but it was still enough and goal difference carried us ahead of Sheffield United to the title.

Some of the scenes among the supporters were disappointing, after all the work Howard Wilkinson and the directors had put in. They were trying to educate the fans, as well as lift the club back up by its bootlaces. Success on the field was vital, but off the field was almost equally important to the men who were re-shaping the whole Elland Road set-up. It was unfortunate that the fixture list had had us there on Bank Holiday weekend, and maybe better planning by the League would have helped us avoid the trouble there was. I am not trying to defend anyone who did cause trouble – we don't want them following the club. Leeds suffered badly before because of a hooligan element which attached itself to the team. Luckily the incidents at Bournemouth seemed to be a one-off. And that was a relief to us all.

One of my dreams came true that day, of course. I had wanted to help revitalise one of the giants of the game. That had been a dream for years, and when I was leaving Old Trafford it was at the forefront of my thinking. Howard Wilkinson had given me the chance to do it and now it had all worked out. I had never had any regrets about not joining Big Ron and teaming up with him again, but, if I had done, then the win at Bournemouth would have wiped them away.

However, if I had had doubts at the beginning about winning promotion, these same doubts surfaced in the summer again – my time for worrying. Would we be good enough to stay up? Would I last the pace in a return to the First Division? The answers came during that first year back and I realised that I had worried unduly. We had more new players as the manager again raided the transfer market and bought so shrewdly. The touch of class provided by the likes of Gary McAllister gave another dimension to our play.

We reached the semi-finals of the Rumbelow's Cup only to lose to Manchester United – a result which hurt me personally, as it would have been a nice little feeling to turn my old club over. Still, we did get to that late stage of the competition and we finished fourth in the League, well ahead of several of the more fancied sides. It was the progress that Howard Wilkinson had asked from us when the season opened. There had been no far-off targets this time, no win or bust feeling about the place. You felt that he wanted time to establish the team, and then we could go from there.

I still have that gut feeling. Howard won't rest until he takes Leeds back to the top. Being in the First Division is only part of the way for him. He will want to take the team to trophy wins and into Europe. He will want to see Leeds restored as one of the giants in English football. Winning that Second Division title was simply a stepping stone for him and for the club. He wants so much more, and I hope that I can still help him do what he wants.

I know this – I was lucky enough to be in at the start of something big. I was there at Pittodrie when Aberdeen took off. Leeds can be the same. They have the players, they have the manager and they have ambitious men behind the club. The Chairman, Mr Silver, gives Howard Wilkinson the kind of backing that every manager needs. He gives him money when he needs it. He treats the players well. But, most important of all, he backs the manager's judgment all the way. You can't ask for more than that.

That is the kind of base bosses dream of. The set-up is right. The club is bigger than outsiders realise and they are going places.

VINNY AND THE CULT OF THE PERSONALITY

WHILE WE WERE WINNING PROMOTION FROM THE
Second Division in my first full season at Elland Road we were still
finding it difficult to win friends. The image of the club had been
badly damaged in the past and I knew soon after my arrival at Leeds
that we would have a difficult job convincing the football public that
we should be liked. As I have written in another chapter, I had not
realised until my move just how hated Leeds were – and I don't think
I am exaggerating the feelings against us.

For example, I can remember in that promotion season going to
play a very important game against West Ham at Upton Park. We
won 1-0, West Ham had FOUR players booked and yet we were
slaughtered by the London Press. It was hard to accept, but that
was the legacy we had inherited from previous teams and previous
troubles.

Of course there is always a problem when you travel to London to
meet West Ham because you are expected to go there and play the
game the way they like to play it. You are supposed to knock it
around nicely, just tip-tap the ball around the field and don't, for
heaven's sake, challenge anyone too strongly. Well, we went there
determined that we would win the game and that we would play the
way we wanted to play. It was our view that if we fell into the trap
of playing their kind of soccer, then we would be doing exactly what
the opposition wanted. It would also have weakened our own pattern
of play. I have to admit that we did not care too much that day
whether the West Ham fans admired our play or not – getting the
points for promotion was our priority.

It was not a case of trying to prove that we were the most
attractive football team in the Second Division. All we wanted to do
was win in our own way, and by winning, help ensure that we would
be in the First Division the following season. But the victory was not

welcomed in London, as you would expect. What I did not expect, though, was that we would be destroyed in the newspapers, especially as we didn't pick up a single caution. They were the team who had players in trouble. It was all a hangover from the past, though we did have a problem which was of our own making. He was called Vinny Jones and he did nothing to delight the purists at Upton Park. Or at any other ground in the country when I think of it!

But Vinny by now was a personality. Don't ask me how that happened because it's difficult to explain – but it was media hype that turned Vinny into a cult figure. It happened and it was a phenomenon which could only have occurred in English football at that time. I believe that he was bought by the club to do a specific job and that was to help us get out of the Second Division. He didn't have to be the best liked player around. He just had to do the business for the team – although there were times when I did not approve of some of the things he did on the field. I told him so, and the other players told him as well. So did the manager and I believe Vinny Jones was a better player when he left the club than he was when he signed for the Second Division promotion campaign.

The problem, though, is that he did not fit the image of the club that Howard Wilkinson was trying to build. Sadly, Vinny fitted the identikit pictures that too many opposition fans had from the old days. The bad, old days when Leeds were the great unloved of English football.

I think, if I remember correctly, that Vinny said in his book that Gordon Strachan thought that he was 'crap' when he first saw him play. As a matter of fact I didn't think he was as good as that! But he did improve in the time he was at Leeds – both in his ability and in his behaviour. I suppose we are like chalk and cheese but I enjoyed his company and he was a great influence in the dressing-room. He was popular with the lads.

Seriously, it was fun in some ways to be playing with him during that promotion season. He was a good trainer and the fans loved him. They gave him a tremendous reception when he came back to Elland Road to play against us for Sheffield United. I think they appreciated that Vinny had made an important contribution towards our winning promotion to the First Division. And there is no arguing that he did do that. Certain types of player are required to help a team win promotion, and Vinny was one of them. He had tremendous physical strength. He had marvellous commitment to the club's cause. And,

In action in the First Division again

above all, he had this intimidating personality which he could stamp on games. Opposing players don't want to tangle with Vinny if they can help it. Also, given time and space, he can be a good player for any team and he can get goals from midfield because he has a ferocious shot. The trouble with Vinny is that the hard man image, the bovver boy reputation, takes over and, while off the field he is a smashing bloke there are times on the field when he takes liberties.

Yet, despite all of the trouble he gets himself into, he was never sent off while he played for Leeds United. He was booked a couple of times but that was it. I do believe that the way the club is being run, with an example being set by all the players and the policy coming from the top and going all the way through, helped him.

He joined Leeds in the close season, a few months after I had signed. I had come across him before while he was making his fearsome reputation at Wimbledon but I had not had any problems with him – not directly. But I did wonder at the time if he was going to be able to fit into the strict disciplinary code which the Boss laid down.

When we played in a pre-season match in Belgium against their champions, Anderlecht, I thought all my worst fears were going to be realised. Now, this was a friendly, a nice little warm-up game for the two clubs before their respective domestic seasons kicked off. It started off that way too, and for the first twenty minutes nothing much happened and Vinny hadn't even kicked the ball yet. Then from behind me I heard this thud and Vinny trotted by me grinning all over his face. "Well, that's the first one of the season," he said. I looked round and there was this Belgian lad with his nose all over his face and blood everywhere. It was suddenly and painfully obvious to me what had happened. Vinny has just done him. I couldn't believe it. I thought to myself this is not what we need at this club. This is really not what we need at all.

What had happened was there had been a throw-in and the ball had been cleared upfield. Vinny had whacked the opposition player in the face and the ball had not even reached him. No one saw it and Vinny escaped Scot-free, but it left a nasty taste in my mouth and I wondered how he was going to change his ways.

I wasn't the only person unhappy about that dark side of Vinny's game. The manager soon told him that we did not expect that kind of hooliganism on the field. As well as that, I and the rest of the players told him that we did not like that kind of behaviour. We all impressed on him that if he did anything stupid and had himself sent off then he would be affecting the team and letting down all the lads he was playing with, as well as the club. On a practical level he was going to be no use at all to the team and our promotion drive, if he was kicking his heels in the stand serving out suspensions. Nor was he going to help any if he had us down to ten men in an important game just because he had had a rush of blood to the head. On an equally important level we were desperately trying to improve the image of the club and Vinny's tough guy tactics would ruin that. I think, eventually, we all got through to him.

His discipline gradually improved. He did not get himself suspended. He did not give away too many free kicks in areas which could have had us in trouble and he was a better all round player because of these changes. His trouble was that because he had become a personality in the game, he felt he had to live up to all his publicity. All of that had been about how tough he was, how much a macho figure he was and how no one would dare face up to him on the field. This scowling, growling portrait he presented to the world had made him a cult figure. But it also landed him in the kind of trouble which could have been so easily avoided. Vinny committed fouls to show people just how much of a hard man he could be. It didn't make any sense, but it was what people had come to expect, and it was almost as if he felt he had to oblige his public.

The other side of the coin was that he scored some cracking goals and he did help us out in a season where we needed a different type of player from the ones we have now that we are established in the First Division. Don't let anyone kid you about that Second Division – it is a very, very difficult League to escape from. Vinny had the resilience we needed. He did growl at some of the opposition. Sometimes they froze and some of the rest of us were given room to play.

He is a frightening looking guy but he is a funny man too, and he can laugh at himself. I don't mind playing against him now because while I'm sure he will attempt to intimidate me, I know that he would not go out of his way to deliberately hurt me. Anyhow, I have heard all the threats before, and they don't worry me when I'm out on the field. Besides, I know Vinny's secret – he can really be a big softie.

You know, we had a lot of laughs that season even though it was a gruelling one because we were trying to reach the promotion target the Boss had set for us. Vinny often provided us with the laughs because he could be wound up so easily. That could sometimes be

This was close to the end of the season – you can tell by how tired I look in this shot

turned to our advantage. I can remember using that one day when we were playing Middlesbrough at Ayresome Park.

The dressing-room atmosphere that day was a bit too light-hearted for my liking. It was as if we were getting ready to play some kind of bounce game, where the result didn't matter. I knew that we had to keep producing results if we were to get promotion, without having to go through the extra demands of the play-offs. So I thought I would liven things up a little, and Vinny was just the man to get the whole mood changed.

I went out of the dressing-room for a couple of minutes and then came back in and told Vinny that I had heard two of their midfield players bad-mouthing him. I just said to him that these two, Mark Brennan and Trevor Putney, had been saying that if they could not play against Vinny and Batty (our other midfield man, David Batty, who has now played for England) then they couldn't play against anyone. Well, he started kicking tables and doors and punching the walls and suddenly we were up for the game and there was no way that the fellow Putney – the player he was marking – was going to be allowed to play. In fact he didn't kick a ball, Vinny made sure of that. Then, with about ten minutes to go, when we were winning 2-0 and I was congratulating myself on the way it had all worked out, the whole thing almost rebounded on me. Vinny suddenly slapped the other lad, Brennan, on the head and turned to me and asked, "What was he saying about me before the game, wee man?" The Middlesbrough lad just stood there looking totally bewildered by all of this. I mumbled something and moved off in another direction before the story had to be explained.

There is no doubt that Vinny arrived at the club with bad habits and no doubt, either, that he revelled in his reputation. That was what finally led to him leaving and making a move to Sheffield United, where he teamed up with his old Wimbledon boss, Dave Bassett.

You see, Vinny was a personality. He had become a celebrity and when he was left out of the team that was no use to him. He had to be in the spotlight for whatever reasons.

By the time we had gone into the First Division the Manager had gone into the transfer market and spent a million pounds to bring Gary McAllister from Leicester City. It was a sign of the changing face of the club. Other signings were made that summer and then there were others made after our first season back in the top flight. It was an obvious policy or strategy that Howard Wilkinson had been working on. Build a team to win promotion. Change that team around to consolidate in the First Division. And change again in a bid to push the club among the honours.

It was the right way to approach things but there had to be casualties, and Vinny was one of them. At the start of our first year back in the First Division, Vinny could not get a game. Gary was in and the style of football that the manager now wanted left Vinny very much out in the cold. To be fair he had to move on. Vinny realised that for himself. He knew that his celebrity status could not be maintained sitting on the subs' bench. He knew that he had to be in action week in and week out, so he said he wanted a transfer and he was sold to the team which had won promotion alongside us.

I like to think that Vinny enjoyed his football better when he was with us than he had done before moving to Elland Road. I genuinely believe he was a better player when he was sold, after spending a year with the club. His contribution towards winning promotion was tremendously important and, honestly, Vinny, you're much better than 'crap'. You are a whole lot better than an awful lot of people will ever give you credit for!

Yes, I do have Bananas!

I'VE TAKEN A LITTLE BIT OF RIBBING OVER THE DIET I have used to help increase my fitness levels over the past few years. Because it became more or less public knowledge that I now eat a lot of bananas people seemed to think it was a bit of a joke. It is probably the case because until the last few years footballers have not been particularly careful about their diets. Most of the time you would have players eating well-done steaks with maybe a change before a game when some would have a piece of fish or chicken. The odd one would have baked beans on toast, but that was looked on as a bit quirky – just as bananas are today. I don't see it that way obviously.

I've always trained well, and I've always prided myself on my fitness, but the change in my diet only came within the past few years – and it has worked for me. I may be well into my thirties now, but I feel as fit as I have ever done and I put a lot of that down to watching carefully what I eat.

Take the bananas, for example. I was watching the tennis on television one day and I saw Ivan Lendl eating one during a break in his game. I thought to myself, if he is doing that then it must be because it's good for him and will be providing him with the energy he needs to compete at top level. When you check it out you find that bananas have a high vitamin count, containing vitamins A, B and C. They are very nutritious and yet low in calories – in fact ideal for any sportsman.

So now I breakfast every day on bananas and porridge. I put them both in the same bowl, and that's my start to the day. It's a high energy, low fat beginning and I try to keep that kind of healthy eating every day and right through the week. Some days I might have a light lunch but it's not something that I need, because the breakfast gives you the kind of kick start to the day that you need. I cannot remember the last time I ate any chips or fried food – or any kind of junk food at all. I have tried to ease myself away from the kind of meals which I felt were not be doing me any good.

To be honest, I don't think British footballers have paid nearly enough attention to their diet over the years. You take a close look at the players who have been to Italy. Ray Wilkins, Joe Jordan and Graeme Souness come to mind, and they look well. They look fit and they all look as if they could still be playing. The lads who have stayed at home here don't always look as good, and when you speak to them you learn that part of it is down to the diet the clubs suggest for the players. Obviously, in Italy, there is a heavy bias in favour of pasta dishes because that is a carbohydrate which gives you energy quickly, but which is also burned off just as quickly without leaving weight problems in its wake. And so the meals I eat now also use a lot of pasta. I'll have tagliatelle or spaghetti, and with that I'll have tuna fish or prawns or maybe chicken. Occasionally I'll have sautéed meat with pasta but I don't eat as much red meat as I used to.

On match days I have the same breakfast as always, with tea, never coffee – I always take tea now. Then around midday I have a fresh fruit salad and that's it until after the match is over. During the week if I do eat lunch, then it's a case of some toast and paté. When I think back to my young days as a player when we were in digs, you would eat anything before a match because you always seemed to be starving. I'd even eat a steak before playing – and that is crazy.

I don't drink a great deal either. Again, when I was young player I didn't worry about having a few drinks during the week. That's changed. Maybe meeting Alex Ferguson when I was twenty-two helped convince me that boozing was not good for me. Seriously, though, I have learned that. I don't touch spirits at all and I don't touch wine and so I am limited to having just a few beers anyway. I'm not really a drinker and while I can enjoy going out with the lads after a game I just know that while I'm still playing football, drinking is not good for me. So I'll have a social drink on a Saturday night and that is my limit.

It has taken a long time for people to consider their diet in this country but I think more and more players are beginning to look after themselves in this way. And I believe that some of the top clubs are also guiding the players in the right direction. It's important – in fact I don't think you can overestimate just how vital a healthy diet can be to any athlete.

Diet is not the only consideration of course when you are trying to stay fit enough to compete with younger players in the First Division.

I'm lucky because I have always got a great kick out of hard work. I know that there are players who cut down on their training schedules when they have games coming up and maybe that works for them. I don't see how it would because if you are playing in a game which lasts ninety minutes then I don't think short, sharp training work-outs will do you any good. When you are getting older then I think that is even more true. I have felt that myself and I found at Leeds that my thinking is on the same wavelength as the manager's. Basically I believe you have to work just as hard as you can. That way you don't have any problems even with the advancing years!

Over the last few seasons, I have never felt tired or unable to compete in the last twenty minutes of any games I've played in. It's never been a problem to me either in the First Division, or at inter- national level with Scotland. And I have not been forced to alter my style to remain fresh for the ninety minutes. I still like to get about the park, and I still do that because I'm given the freedom within the team pattern to move around. You know, when I was about twenty- five I can remember being told that I would have to change my style of play if I was going to last in the game. If I didn't then I would certainly need two young lads alongside me in the middle of the park because by the time I was thirty my legs would have gone. Well, that's not happened. I have not changed the way I play, because this is the way I enjoy playing the game. And my legs haven't gone either because I have looked after myself over the years.

As long as my fitness level remains the same – and there is no sign of it dropping – then I'll continue playing my way. I don't see any need to change. I want to keep training as hard as I know how and I will do all that the other players do. I don't want to have any special treatment because I don't think I need it and I doubt that I would benefit from it. In the close season I have my own fitness régime just to keep in condition. I allow myself a three-week break from work right at the end of the season. Then, after that, I start off doing five- mile runs every second day. I just set my own pace and then step it up a little as we get closer to the start of the season. I don't think you ever lose your skills – but you can lose your fitness. And when you lose that then you cannot use your skills effectively.

Quite apart from the changes I have made in my lifestyle, I think that my fitness has benefited from the way I have trained hard right through my career. Even as a young lad with Dundee I worked and I didn't dodge training. I try to impress that on younger players at the club today. I tell them that when they are working hard in training it's not just for the game which is coming up the following Saturday – it's for their whole future. Sometimes they don't listen but they should because I'm getting the pay off now from the training I did as a kid. And the training they get today is much better and far more imaginative than when I first came into the game. Pre-season training then was a cross-country run to kick off and that was supposed to find out which players had looked after themselves during the summer. Not too many of them did at that time.

But the training methods were there as if they had been written on tablets of stone. You knew what to expect every single boring day . . . but you still did it.

There is much more thought put into things now because younger managers have picked up on fresh ideas, different ways to approach fitness. Most of it is a whole lot more sensible than it was twenty years ago. Take golf, for instance. In my early days there were regular golf outings for the players organised by the clubs – maybe that still happens at some clubs. But in my book all it does is harm the players, and I'm talking here as someone who enjoys the game. I played my share of it during the football season while I was with Aberdeen but I would never do it now. In fact, I've banned myself from the golf course except when I'm on holiday in the summer. There are too many matches being played now – you are looking at sixty and seventy games a season – to waste any of your available energy on another sport entirely. I mean that. If you go out golfing and you walk off a course exhausted then you have left vital energy out there that you could be using to do your job.

I can remember when Graeme Souness arrived at Rangers as manager and he banned the players from playing golf during the week when the season was in full swing. He was criticised, and some of the players had a bit of a moan, but he was dead right. If I ever become a manager I would do exactly the same thing!

If a footballer goes out on to a golf course for three or four hours carrying a golf bag, he is using up energy which could be put to use in training harder. Or playing harder!

The hours spent tramping round a golf course could be put to better use. They could help you be a fitter player and, therefore, a better player. I cannot understand how footballers can gamble with their energy the way that they do. It is vital that energy is preserved and used for the game itself. I gave up golfing during the season quite

You'll only see me in this pose in the summer now . . . because I've banned myself from playing golf during the season

readily. It was no big deal, certainly it was no hardship. I enjoyed playing the game, but I don't see the point in having a game of pleasure interfere with what I do for a living – and I think golf does that.

A modern footballer has to be an athlete. You cannot get by in today's game by standing around for most of the ninety minutes and then knocking balls here and there when you happen to get possession. That is no longer enough, not nearly enough. Times have changed and attitudes with them. You don't have footballers arriving back from a long hot summer in the sun, well over-weight and collapsing halfway round the track during the pre-season work-outs. When I was a young player, the lads would be like cripples after the first week of pre-season training. Everyone would have blisters and every-one would be exhausted. Everyone would also be complaining. It's not like that any longer. Very few players report back after the summer break even slightly over-weight. One reason is that the close

I have trained hard throughout my career. Here I am with the Scotland team before the international with England in 1980. (Picture: Daily Record)

season is shorter now, but the other is that players are taking care of themselves much better than they used to. The game is so much faster now that you have to maintain your fitness levels. If you fail to do that then you won't make it in any of the top League sides.

I don't want to come over here like some fitness freak. It's just that I try to be sensible and I think that's why I lasted this long in the game. I honestly thought that by the time I was thirty I would be trudging around with an insurance book or something similar – instead I was able to kick off another career at Leeds. And as long as I'm fit enough to keep going then that's what I'll do. The manager took assessments of the players' fitness when we came back to re-start training last summer. He told me then that I was still in the top four at the club and that was encouraging. It doesn't suggest I'm too old, does it? Doesn't suggest that I'm ready for the knacker's yard yet! There are fifty or so players at the club – all of them younger

than me – and I'm still among the leaders in terms of all-round fitness. So I guess I must be doing something right.

As well as diet and training, I am into bio-kinetics and I have my own masseur, or at least, there is this expert in the field, a Norwegian called Harold Oyen, who looks after me. If I have anything wrong with me then I speak to Harold about it and he can help. I'm not saying that what he preaches and practises will work for everyone – but it has done wonders for me. He works on stress management and I met him while I was still at Old Trafford. I got to know him through the Manchester United director and former player Bobby Charlton, who was endorsing seaweed tablets. Harold was in contact with Bobby and I was fascinated by his ideas on fitness. I began to use his methods and I feel that they have given me something extra, just that little bonus which helps keep my energy levels high. It makes me feel better. And fitter. And healthier. That's all that counts.

To try to explain this as simply as possible, and tell you my understanding of the subject, bio-kinetics says that there is a flow of energy which runs through your body and if you are to be at your peak physically then the flow must be kept going properly and be balanced. The theory is that you can maintain the right balances by fingertip pressure applied to various points just as some people use acupuncture. Only with this you don't have any needles – you use only your fingertips. I've seen it referred to as acupressure and that, I suppose, is fairly accurate.

The belief is that if one muscle, or one part of your body, is out of balance then you are in trouble. If a muscle is damaged or if it is over-active then your whole body can be put out of sync. When you apply pressure then you can restore the proper balance. You keep the balances right by this fingertip pressure. I can do this, to some extent, for myself now and I have a little ritual that I go through in the dressing-room before training and before games. I sit there and give myself a little massage in certain places. When I first got to Leeds I think some of the players must have thought I was potty. They must have taken a look at me sitting there pushing and prodding away at these different pressure points and thought: "We've got a right one here!"

Eventually someone had the courage to speak up and ask me what the hell I thought I was doing and I explained to them. After that Lee Chapman and Chris Fairclough gave it a go and it seemed to help them – Lee scored a right few goals, so it must have been good!

After joining Leeds I played one hundred and twenty games on the trot and missed just seventeen minutes! That can't be bad for someone in his thirties. It's no miracle treatment. You cannot go out drinking every night and then expect Harold to come along and give you this fingertip massage and then you'll be OK. You'll not be the perfect athlete after a half-hour treatment. It doesn't work that way. It's not magic. What it does is enhance your fitness – but you have to have a good level of fitness to begin with. You have to eat right, train right and sleep right and then with the bio-kinetics you can make yourself five or ten per cent fitter than you are already. That can give you an edge on your opponent in a game and that is what you are always looking for – just that little bit extra that can make you come out on top.

So every couple of weeks Harold comes through to see me and give me a thorough going over. He is an incredible man. He visits regularly to keep my muscle balance right and he knows when there is anything wrong – just by doing his little bit of massage he can tell you what is troubling you. If it's an injury he can tell you where it is. Sometimes he can sense damage which has not yet surfaced. I can tell you a story to illustrate that. One day he came to my home to give me the treatment and the night before – a Saturday – I had been out and had had a few beers. Now, as I said earlier, I can't drink much and I don't drink very often. But this Sunday I felt under the weather, just a little bit rough. I didn't say anything to him about it. I didn't have to. Within a few minutes he said to me: "You were drinking last night." I owned up that I had been out after the game and asked him how he knew. "Oh," he told me, "your liver is over-active and I'll have to balance that out." And he did!

I believe that by keeping that energy flow properly balanced I can avoid serious injury. If you are not one hundred per cent fit then you pick up knocks much more easily than if you are at your peak. I've been lucky that I haven't had too many really bad injuries and not many players are going to be able to say that in the years to come. We play too much football now, and the games are faster and more physical than before. The demands are different now. Do you know that ten years ago no one in the game had ever had a hernia operation? Yet they are now commonplace. I was the second player to have one and the specialist explained to me what had happened. He told me that when you need a hernia operation, it is your body telling you that enough is enough – it's like a car blowing a gasket. It cannot

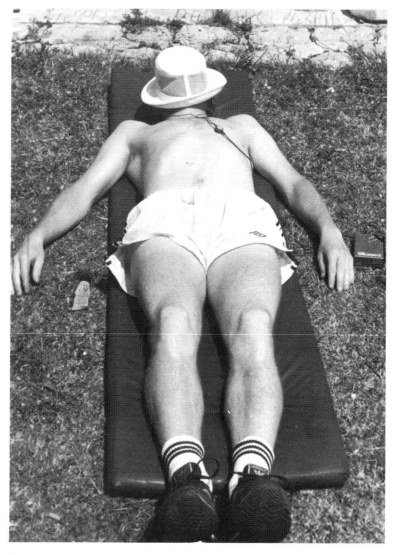

I don't want to come over as a fitness freak, so here's a shot of me at rest!
(Picture: *Daily Record*)

stand the strain any longer. That's what your body is saying to you when you need that operation. The number of Achilles injuries that you get today are also caused by stress. That is why the levels of fitness have to be that much higher than they were in previous times. The bottom line is that to exist in the game you must be an athlete.

Oh, in all this fitness talk, I forgot the simplest thing of all – REST. I picked up on that from Kenny Dalglish and you could not find a better example of any professional than Kenny. He looked after himself and one of the things he made sure of was that he had plenty of rest. I used to see him go off to his bed in the afternoon when we were together with Scotland. Most of the lads would be in the snooker room at the hotel. Or some of them would be watching the racing on the box. Or we would be having a game of putting, or even taking a sauna. Not Kenny – none of that was for him. When he had free time, usually in the afternoon when the training and the team talks were over, he was off to his bed for a couple of hours. Soon I was following his example. I reasoned it out this way – if it's good enough for Kenny then it's got to be good enough for me. Willie Miller was another who began to go for these afternoon naps and I'm still doing it whenever I can. It works wonders for you.

But it's when you take these things I have discussed here and put them all together that you can reap the benefits. The demands on the modern footballer are fierce and seem to be growing fiercer every season. To match them you have to be fit. That means eating right, training right and resting as often as you can. And if you can find your own Harold Oyen then you're quids in.

The Blunder which Almost Wrecked my Career

I CAN STILL REMEMBER THE DAY IN THE SUMMER OF 1984 when I agreed to join Manchester United – indeed, it's a day I'll never forget. But for all the wrong reasons!

That was the day when I believed that a signing blunder I had made would wreck the move to Old Trafford. Maybe even wreck the whole of my career.

All of this was because of one of my famous rows with Alex Ferguson, or, at least partly because of that. We had always had our moments, Alex and I, in the years we were together at Aberdeen. It didn't seem to matter that these were among the best years of both of our football lives – we still clashed frequently.

That particular season our feuding was even more frequent and furious than ever before. I suppose deep down we each knew that we were coming to the end of the line, that my time with Aberdeen was over, and that I had to get a transfer away from Pittodrie to continue my career elsewhere. On my part I was nervous, uncertain about the future and edgy about being constantly in the limelight, as it was public knowledge that my contract ended in the summer. It was a difficult time, and Alex, who basically understood that I had to move on, was not ready to accept that his team might start to break up.

The bottom line was that while we understood each other's situation we were destined to be on a collision course all the way through that season. The situation wasn't helped by the pressures which surrounded the side that year. As we entered the second half of the season we were going for a treble – the Premier League title, the Scottish Cup and the European Cup Winners Cup, the trophy we had won the previous season. Alex, being Alex, wanted them all, and the last thing that he needed was one player upsetting his plans due to off-the-field concerns.

In a small way we had been down this road before, when I stupidly asked for a transfer after returning from the World Cup in Spain two years earlier. That was eventually smoothed over and, to be honest, I knew that I had been out of order. I was under contract for two more years and I should have been prepared to honour that deal. In some ways that little bit of trouble became a dress rehearsal for the real thing.

This time, though, I was well within my rights to decide to move on. My contract was ending and Aberdeen had not been able to make me the kind of offer which might have persuaded me to stay. Mind you, I doubt if any offer would have kept me because by then I felt that I had to get away from the monotony of the Premier League. I needed a break from that grind where you must meet all the top clubs at least FOUR times each season but where, in reality, you often meet them SIX or even SEVEN times. It was a problem I had lived with through the years at Aberdeen, but I felt worn out by it now.

So as the season neared its climax the situation at the club was becoming more and more tense, more and more frayed. I knew that I was leaving but I had no idea where my future was going to be. Suddenly my whole life seemed disorganised. For years I had had a future to look forward to, and the successes with Aberdeen had kept the prospects looking good. Now, in theory, they should be better but the uncertainty gnawed away at me. It was a traumatic time for me and I'm sure other players have found it to be the same. It is very hard to focus your mind properly and put all your attention on the games you are playing when your entire future is up in the air.

If I ever become a manager and find myself in a similar situation with a top player, then I think I would leave him out. I don't believe that anyone can perform 100 per cent when their mind is constantly leaping away to the future and the possibilities that loom ahead. It is a pretty impossible situation, and while there will be players who can handle all of these different pressures, I don't think that I was one of them. Not at that time anyway.

Probably Alex Ferguson made mistakes too, because this was the first time he had encountered the freedom of contract problem with one of his top players. He must have looked at all the fuss being made of me and wondered how it was affecting his other players. Obviously he had to look at the whole affair from a different viewpoint than mine. He had Aberdeen Football Club to think about – not only Gordon Strachan.

Happy days with Aberdeen as I give a big hand to the fans.
(Picture: *Daily Record*)

He had three trophies he wanted to win and he had to protect the future of the club. He didn't want to waste too much time on a player who was going to turn his back on all he had built at Pittodrie. Yet, at the same time, he clearly felt that a balance had to be struck, that a compromise had to be worked out. He did not want to leave me out if that was going to weaken his challenge in the three tournaments.

Now, looking back, I think the team was actually better prepared than Alex thought at the time. Perhaps if he had left me out of the team it would have helped the mental agonies I was suffering. Probably I felt as he did that my absence would cause problems – now I reckon we were both wrong. There was a lot of experience in that team. A lot of trophies had been won and a lot of crises had been overcome. There was an organisation and resilience in the squad which would have prevented one player from causing too much of an upset.

But back then it wasn't easy to see that. There was too much bickering between the pair of us to look at anything logically. The smallest thing could cause a great deal of friction. Just the slightest comment I might make in a newspaper about a move, and Fergie would fly off the handle. Yet it was almost impossible for me to stay silent, because every day there was more speculation about the clubs who seemed ready to move in and sign me. OK, I should have kept my mouth shut some of the time but it was very difficult – even though I could sense that Alex was fed up with the media attention I was getting. It needled him.

I didn't blame him for feeling that way. It was only natural and I'm sure I would have felt the same. It is never a good thing at any club to place all the focus on one individual ahead of the rest of the team. It is a helluva situation for a manager to be in. What does he do? Does he ignore what is happening even though he thinks it might be affecting the morale of the other players? Or does he try to bring the centre of this attention – in this case, yours truly – down a peg or two in front of the others? There is no easy decision, no simple choice, and the way it worked with us was that we simply argued our way through the whole messy business.

I think it was the worst time I have known in my whole career. I suffered in the Dundee reserve team, and again in the second string at Pittodrie, when I wondered if I was ever going to make it as a player. But this was worse because there were days and even weeks when I could see no end to the problems which eventually engulfed me.

Freedom of contract has been a tremendous breakthrough for players but as in any other change, problems are bound to surface in its wake. So I would find myself trying to rest on a Friday afternoon before an important game when the phone would ring, and an agent from the Continent – or from here in Britain – would be on the other end with promises of untold riches. Just about every club in Europe and England seemed to want me according to these calls. The promises that were made were astonishing. Then, with all that on your mind, you had to get yourself into Pittodrie and get yourself ready for whatever game you faced on the Saturday afternoon. You'd been up half the night with your mind racing back and forward over all the possibilities and you still had to perform week after week. There would be cars on offer and houses and more money than I'd ever dreamed of. And I'd find myself sitting in the dressing-room before a game and saying to Mark McGhee, "What about this offer, Dingus, the one I got last night?" and the game would be looming. It was a terrible time and one I could not adjust to properly. Before

This picture of me with Gavin was taken back in 1984, when it was still unclear which jersey he'd be swopping his Aberdeen one for. (Picture: *Daily Record*)

all of it happened I had always felt that I could divide my mind, compartmentalise my thoughts so that one did not intrude on the other. But I found out the hard way that I could not do that.

I'll own up now – I did not give enough mentally to the team in those last few months of that season. I gave everything I could physically, but I simply couldn't handle all the pressures which overwhelmed me. It's to the credit of the rest of the team that, while my mind was darting all over the place, they were able to buckle down and win the League and Cup double that season. I thought at the time I was giving it my best shot but I wasn't.

Despite it all, despite my personal turmoil and my feuds with the manager, it turned into a good season for us. It should have been a good season for me to say my farewells – another Premier League Championship, another Scottish Cup victory and a semi-final spot in the European Cup Winners Cup. Talk about going out on a high!

And yet, personally, I just wish it had all happened so differently. It would have been so much better if the transfer had just gone through quietly at the end of the season without all the fuss beforehand. Unhappily that's not possible in these days of contract freedom. You have those few months when everyone in football knows you have to make up your mind, and the spotlight is on you until that decision is made. There is no way to get round that problem, it seems.

Certainly, the way I tried to short circuit the whole ongoing circus was the wrong one. It almost finished me as a footballer. It also put my eventual move to Manchester United – the club I had dreamed about joining – under serious threat. Seven years on I can't believe how stupid I was. But it all happened, and it was down to me and no one else. I have to carry the can for the biggest mistake I have ever made.

Think about this. Here I am with freedom of contract looming and all kinds of clubs ready to bid, and I put my name to agreements with TWO Continental clubs – one in Italy and one in West Germany. All of this happening without Aberdeen's knowledge, and without Alex Ferguson's knowledge!

The one which caused me the biggest headache was the one I signed for Cologne, the Bundesliga club who became very determined that I would play my football with them – or, if not, then finish up playing for no one at all. That was the kind of threat which hung over my head as the end of the season approached and was still there when the Manchester United bid was accepted by Aberdeen.

It all happened because of another fall out I had with Alex Ferguson. This time the blow-up between us came during the build-up to the game in Portugal where we were playing Porto in the semi-final first leg of the Cup Winners tournament. He had mentioned something about a transfer in the team hotel and I took the spur. It was my turn to be upset because I felt he was getting at me unfairly on this occasion. Of course, this kind of thing was happening all the time. I think the rest of the players found it all a bit of a joke. But neither Alex nor I could find anything at all funny about the situation.

So, after the game there was an agreement offered to me on behalf of the Cologne club and I signed. The one thing in my favour here is that this was not an official signing-on document issued by the West German FA. It was a letter of intent, if you like, which stated that I would join Cologne when my contract with Aberdeen ended. The get-out I thought I had was that I was under the impression that this only affected me IF I decided that I wanted to play the rest of my football in the Bundesliga. The trouble came when Cologne insisted that the agreement was binding. They wanted to hold me to it.

Now, Verona were different. They accepted that the agreement only applied if I wanted to play football in Italy. Otherwise they were happy to tear the piece of paper up. In fact, when I agreed to sign for United the Verona people sent me a letter of congratulation. They also called to ask me whom they should sign as my replacement when they finally grasped the fact that I was going to Old Trafford.

Cologne, though, took the whole business right down to the wire. They claimed that the agreement was legal, recognised by their association and by the European Union. They wanted me to join them and they were determined to block the move to Old Trafford if they possibly could. They claimed that they had built all their plans around my being there and playing for them in the new season. They also said that they had used my signing to persuade their other top players – including World Cup goalkeeping star Harald Schumacher – to stay on with the club when their contracts were ending. They also maintained that they had called off their hunt for a midfield player because I had agreed to join them and, now that I had changed my mind, they had missed out on the opportunity of signing another player of international class.

It was a mess! And I was slap bang in the middle of it all. It was the worst kind of nightmare and all the possible consequences were laid out in front of me.

Cologne threatened to sue me for breach of contract, citing what they believed my change of heart had cost them, with regard to having, perhaps, to pay out an inflated sum for an in-contract player to take over the role which had been waiting for me to fill in their team.

Cologne also threatened to have me banned from playing any football at all, until the contract wrangle was sorted out – and that might have taken a whole season. It had turned into the most troubled and complicated time of my life, when all I had started out to do was look after the future of my wife and my family. At that time I was twenty-seven years old and I was convinced that this transfer was going to be the one which would give me the opportunity to safeguard my life after the game, after I had finished playing. I saw it as my last chance to do all of this – though circumstances changed for me when Leeds resurrected my career five years further on. But then, I regarded this as the contract which would see out my career. Now that career was being threatened with an earlier end than I'd had in mind.

At the time of the dispute I was angry at Cologne and the way they handled the whole business. Now, though, I understand them better. I also feel a little sorry for them, because if it had been any other club other than Manchester United which had come on the scene, then I would have gone to West Germany and relished a future in the Bundesliga. It was their bad luck that United had that little bit of magic, that sprinkling of stardust which excited every player of my generation, and probably still excites the youngsters of today.

Strangely enough, after the weeks and months of speculation and fuss which had surrounded me and my future, the actual deal which took me to Old Trafford arrived suddenly. And quietly – or, as quietly as a £500,000 transfer move can be.

I walked into Pittodrie one morning ready to do a spot of training. At this stage there was the usual stony silence between the manager and myself. It had been that way for a while. The shouting matches had gone. All the public rows had faded into the background and now there was just this atmosphere. We had not had a public falling out over the long drawn-out transfer saga, there hadn't been a slanging match for the world to witness. Instead we had settled into this silence and anyone who happened to be around us at the ground knew there was something wrong. There was a definite strain even though we had stopped growling at each other. This morning when I went in he was in the snooker room playing a match as I walked past the door. As I passed he shouted to me, "Martin Edwards wants you to phone him. Give him a ring just now." So I said: "Martin Edwards of Manchester United?" He replied that that was the man and that was the end of our conversation.

He went on to miss the black and I went through to the office to phone Old Trafford.

I had to go to Edinburgh to open a pub for Pat Stanton who had been assistant manager at Aberdeen for a spell. I had promised to do that so I went to Manchester via Edinburgh for the signing talks which were to plunge my life into all that trouble from Cologne.

Another twenty-four hours and there would have been no trouble. I was already booked on a flight to Cologne and I would have signed for them officially if United had not come in. By then I had given up hope of them ever making a move, even though they had been linked with me for months. Anyhow I met Martin Edwards and he ran through everything for me. The deal was marvellous. I was going to join the top club in Britain. Even Alex Ferguson seemed happy now that things had been agreed between the two clubs.

Then I had to tell Mr Edwards about the document which Cologne held with my signature on it. We were shaking hands to clinch the signing when I felt I had to tell him about the complication. He immediately pooh-poohed it. There would be nothing to worry about, he told me. It was not going to be a problem. But, of course, as I have told you, it was. And for a little time it looked as if it was going to be an insurmountable problem for the two clubs, Aberdeen and Manchester United, and for me.

Eventually it was all settled and there was talk of Aberdeen having to pay Cologne a sum of money in compensation but, to be honest, I cannot remember the details. Basically I think I pushed all the events after signing for United to the back of my mind. I was happy to let the clubs sort out the problems I had created for myself. I had not done it out of any malice – it was just naivety on my part coupled, at the time, with that row with the manager.

In fact I would have been a wealthier man if I had taken up Cologne's offer. There was more money on offer in West Germany than there was at Old Trafford. Plus there were other perks which could not have been offered to me by any other club in Britain. But it was not about money alone by this time – it was about the magic of United, something that Alex Ferguson was to succumb to a few years later himself.

When I agreed to join United I did not meet up with Ron Atkinson, the manager – he was in Israel on holiday. It seemed a little strange to me at the time that he could not interrupt his break to sign a half-million-pound player. It was a new experience for me,

Arriving at Manchester Airport with my wife Lesley to meet Manchester United supremo Martin Edwards. If I look a little apprehensive it's because I've still to tell him about "signing" for Cologne!

especially after Pittodrie, where Alex was such a 'hands-on' manager. Nothing happened at that club that Alex did not know about. There was no way in the world that he would not be present when a new player was being signed.

Yet, in spite of my surprise, I found it a refreshing change. Speaking to Martin Edwards at that first meeting when the whole deal was being thrashed out, I knew that I was speaking to the man who mattered at the club as far as financial details were concerned. The way the system worked at Old Trafford then, was that Big Ron identified the players he would like to buy for the club and then the chairman got on with the BUSINESS side of it all. He worked out the fee with the selling club and settled the contract with the new player. This meant that decisions could be made immediately, rather than have people toing and froing behind the scenes – something which is so often the case with a lot of clubs. At Aberdeen any re-signing talks seemed to go on forever because Alex handled them but, obviously, before finalising anything, the chairman Dick Donald had to be consulted. So Alex would approach a player with an offer and the player would ask for something else. That meant Alex had to go back to the chairman to clear that point and then another little point would arise which had to be sorted out too. Naturally other things would come up between times and the re-signing talks would be shelved for a week or two and then be picked up once more. You would eventually find yourself arguing over a fiver a week.

Mind you, Aberdeen was a different set up, a different kind of club and one that prided itself on good housekeeping and sensible financial policies. That was the policy which had brought them success and stability in troubled times for football, so you could not blame them. But it was always as if Alex saw himself as the guardian of the club's finances and it made negotiations very, very difficult.

At United it was simple. Apart from the Cologne trouble, everything went just as it had been promised when I shook hands with Martin Edwards that night. It was a move I never regretted for a moment. I shudder to think how close I had been to messing it up. Probably United are everyone's second favourite team, the team that comes after your home side or whoever you do happen to support. There were only two other clubs in England I would have considered joining – Liverpool and Arsenal. But I knew from the outset that Liverpool had no interest in signing me, and while Arsenal watched me time after time they made no move. Now I'm glad it happened that way because United would always have been my choice.

The only regrets I have over the transfer are those I have set down here. I still feel that something should be done to protect a player whose contract is ending. Something should be done to allow a transfer to take place ONLY at the end of the season and any approaches should be banned until then. If that had been the case when my time with Aberdeen was ending I would have avoided all the agonies which scarred those last few months. Everything would have been done in the proper fashion and I would have signed for

United without the threats from Cologne hanging over me. It WAS my fault. I am not ducking out of my share of responsibility in the matter, but given protection or even better guidance at the time, I would never have landed up in that mess.

Premier League Feuds

THERE WERE MANY REASONS WHY I HAD CHOSEN TO leave Aberdeen and, while it's always the case that fans talk about the money side of things, that is never the only reason.

I'm honest enough to admit that the financial advantages counted for a great deal. I was twenty-seven years old and I wanted security for the future, not only for myself, but also for my family. That is natural. It is surely what any working man would want. But other reasons did come into play and one of these was that I felt I had done as much as I possibly could for Aberdeen. I did not think I was capable of giving any more and I was beginning to feel constricted by the place and by the Premier League.

Deep down I'm sure that Alex Ferguson felt the same as I did – but he could not admit to that. He had to try to keep me. He had to let the support see that the club wanted me to stay. Yet I'm sure if he had examined the situation then he would have agreed that my time was up. In fact, I believe that Alex had reached the opinion that he would not be able to get any more out of me. That happens in a player-manager relationship. There comes a time when over-familiarity doesn't breed contempt, but certainly breeds an awareness of each other's strengths and weaknesses. When that does happen it's usually a time for the parting of the ways because both player and manager know that a lot of motivation is going to be lost.

Don't get me wrong. I loved Aberdeen, I loved the place, I loved the club and I loved the lads. There was a bond between us which I think is still there because we had grown up together at that club. We were all young ambitious players together, we all got married around the same time and then our families began growing up together. On the football side we started to have success at the same time too. But those days were over. We had had the success we had all been searching for. We had the medals to show anyone who doubted our ability.

75

This was a Premier clash – literally – at Love Street against St Mirren in 1982.
(Picture: *Daily Record*)

We had the international caps too – but for me it was time to move, time to look for fresh challenges and different opposition – especially different opposition.

That last season I played in the Premier League we played against Celtic SEVEN times, and the atmosphere surrounding these games was becoming really nasty. By the end of it all we were like the hillies and the billies – just feuding and fighting our way through the games. The whole scene became poisonous. You would be going off the field after a game and a player would be saying to you, "Just you wait, I'll get you the next time." That happens in England too, but the next time is months away and everything is forgotten. In the Premier League the 'next time' could be three weeks off, maybe even less, so you had these troubles lying in wait for you at just about every game. And when you are my size you can do without all of that!

Believe me, I was not enjoying my football any more. I couldn't. I was waiting for someone to hammer me every time I went out on to the field.

When Aberdeen had first been successful under Alex Ferguson we had had a few encounters of the ugly kind with Rangers. That was the Old Guard at Ibrox who were playing then, guys like Alex MacDonald, Colin Jackson and big Tom Forsyth, and these games could be rough and, to say the least, rugged. They were not going to give up the success they had known to a bunch of young players from Pittodrie. I could identify with that and I honestly relished the challenge of those games.

But when the same thing started to happen when we played Celtic I felt bogged down by the same old boring routine. It was also a lot worse than it had been before. There was a nasty feeling about the games and an intensity in those clashes which I simply did not enjoy. I doubt if any player could say with any honesty that he did enjoy these matches. I was running out of arguments on the field and I just wanted to be away from all the bad feeling.

It was more difficult for me being a forward. I can remember Willie Miller saying that to me one day when I was talking about being disillusioned by the Premier League and all the problems we were having – particularly in the Celtic games. Willie pointed out that it was easier to be a defender because they could suss out what the opposing player was going to do and take the appropriate steps to stop him. They learned any attacking player's repertoire of tricks, which foot he preferred, which way he was likely to move, the areas he would prefer to run into. A good defender, said Willie, would know all that about a player within a season. For an attacker, though, it was so different.

I knew Willie was right. If a defender did not get everything right for himself then at least he would have his team's coaches helping him. But as an attacker I had to come up with something fresh every season, if not every game. I felt that I was running out of ideas and I did not like that. I was finding it hard to maintain standards that I had set for myself, hard to add an extra element of surprise to my game after ten years of competing in the Premier League, week after week after weary week.

I was at the stage that to play in a European Cup game or an international match with Scotland was like a breath of fresh air. I had space to play and time to hold the ball and no threats to hold me

Here I am in training for those Premier feuds back in 1981.
(Picture: *Daily Record*)

back. I felt a real deep down need to get out of the Premier League because I had had enough of the kind of football played there and enough of the monotony all players would feel in the confining atmosphere of that set-up. I had to get away. I had to move on and I had to play my football somewhere where there was a chance to breathe, a chance to match myself against new opponents and possibly higher standards.

When the Scottish Cup final came round that season at Hampden, it was the clincher. We played Celtic that day and beforehand the football bosses prepared for trouble. The feeling in the build-up to the final was like no other I had known and it is not something I would want to see repeated. Unhappily the bosses were right. There was trouble and I became involved in it through no fault of my own. If ever I had needed convincing that my decision to quit Scottish soccer was right, then it came that afternoon.

The SFA were criticised for their pre-match attitudes – but looking back maybe they were right. There had been bother in just about every game we played and at the end of the seven games – including that fateful final – there had been THIRTY-TWO bookings and TWO orderings off! If any fixture could be labelled explosive then it was Aberdeen paired with Celtic.

Don't ask me why the bad feeling flared between the two teams, although I suppose it had something to do with the fact that the Old Firm did not relish their long-time dominance of the game in Scotland being not just challenged but taken away. That was the time when ourselves and Dundee United were dubbed the 'New Firm' and I doubt if either Rangers or Celtic liked that.

Also, Alex Ferguson had drummed into us that the two Glasgow giants were favoured by referees, that because of the support they carried with them to every game, officials were initimidated. He encouraged us to question refereeing decisions we felt were dodgy – just as Rangers and Celtic players had done over the years. It was Alex's belief that this had benefited the big two down through the years and he claimed he was speaking from knowledge, having played as a striker for Rangers himself. His argument was that these two clubs pressured referees and that we had to do the same. We had to fight fire with fire, if you like. Previously we had stood back and watched referees being hassled by the Old Firm players – now we were told to get in there and fight for our rights. That was probably another bone of contention with Celtic.

Something I'd rather not remember – a memory of those troubled times between Aberdeen and Celtic. This time I was attacked by a Celtic supporter. Things improved after this – the attacks were only verbal!

They did not like us putting our oar in when there was any argument over decisions. And Alex Ferguson had us fired up for these games. He used to wind us up something rotten. He had us believing that everyone in Glasgow hated us. That was always his theme before we played at Ibrox or at Parkhead. It was always the same story with him – but we believed it because he told it with such intensity. You would go into these games determined to do really well and convinced that everyone – including the referee and the two linesmen – was against you. He told us that their players would try to intimidate the match officials and that we had to stand up for ourselves. "Don't let them get away with anything" was basically his message and so we would take the field expecting injustice. If it came then that would fire us up still further. Meanwhile the divine right to success of the Old Firm was being tossed out of the window and their players and fans didn't like that one little bit. Maybe, looking back, Alex Ferguson was right – the people in Glasgow did hate us!

I suppose we gave them cause. We did follow the guidance given by the manager and we tried our best to neutralise the pressures those other teams exerted on the referees. Above all, we used to win those games a lot more frequently than any Aberdeen team had done in the past. To rub salt into the wounds, of course, ourselves and Dundee United were, more often than not, staying in Europe longer than the two Glasgow sides. There is no doubt that they envied us our success in the European Cup Winners final in Gothenburg when that came.

All of that built up over the seasons until that last season brought a series of explosions – and none bigger than the Cup final storm.

Sensing that the game might boil over, the SFA decided that the two managers, Alex Ferguson of Aberdeen and Davie Hay of Celtic, should attend a meeting at their Park Gardens HQ in the week leading up to the Hampden clash. Their idea was to warn the two team bosses about the responsibility which faced the clubs, the managers and the players in the final. They wanted to emphasise that they did not want a repeat of some of the indiscipline which had occurred in the other six games between us that season.

It was putting an extra burden on us all and Davie Hay made it very plain that he had no need and no desire to attend any such meeting. That set the scene for a series of bad-tempered exchanges between the Celtic manager and the soccer bosses as the build-up to the final got under way. If anything, it aggravated the tensions which all of us knew were there in any case. The last thing we needed was more trouble off the field before we got to the game itself.

After all, there were more than enough problems for us already. This was going to be Celtic's only chance to save their season by winning a trophy. They had beaten us in the two-legged semi-final of the League Cup but had then gone down to Rangers in the final of that tournament. They lost that match 3-2 after extra time and they finished the Premier League programme seven points behind us as we took the title once more. They had beaten us twice in the six games before the final, both times at Parkhead. One of these was the second leg of the League Cup semi-final and the other was the last League game between us when we had the title more or less won and the result did not matter a great deal. Then, while Celtic were plunging out of the UEFA Cup in the third round of the competition against Nottingham Forest we were in the process of winning the European Super Cup by beating Hamburg 2-0 over the two legs. We

Another shot of the mystery Parkhead invader! (Picture: *Daily Record*)

had also reached the last four of the European Cup Winners' Cup which we were defending and so our stock was high while Celtic were struggling. The resentments they felt as a club and also among their fans had grown and grown and now, as the season climaxed, the bitterness they felt towards us could almost be tasted.

The only thing which was going to be right with them that May day was if they won the Cup. It wouldn't have mattered HOW they won it, just as long as they could carry it back in triumph to the east end of Glasgow and place it proudly in the board room at Celtic Park. Losing was unthinkable, especially as this was their solitary chance of a trophy and especially as they had already lost one final that season to their oldest rivals and were now facing up to the team they still thought of as pretenders to their crown.

The backdrop to the game was ominous and when the hugely experienced referee Bob Valentine was given special instructions to warn the players before the game that he would clamp down on any trouble then the writing was on the wall. The SFA bosses were looking for trouble – and unhappily that was what they got. For the first time in fifty-five years a player was ordered off in the Scottish Cup final and to make the matter even worse the man shown the red card was the Celtic captain Roy Aitken.

The last time a man was ordered off was in 1929 when Rangers' Jock Buchanan was given his marching orders against Kilmarnock, who went on to win the trophy by beating the Ibrox team 2-0. I suppose that must have been a sensation at the time – but it could never have brought as much trouble in its wake as this particular incident which saw Big Roy leave the field seven minutes before half time.

When we had won the game by 2-1 after extra time the Celtic board of directors immediately announced that they would be protesting to the SFA. They complained that they were unhappy at referee Bob Valentine's handling of the game. They were also unhappy at pre-match instructions given to the referee by the SFA secretary Ernie Walker. Later Mr Walker denied that he had given any instructions and pointed out that any advice handed to the referee before the final came from the chairman of the Referee Supervisors, Jack Mowat, and that was done prior to every final.

In the war of words which followed, Celtic boss Davie Hay insisted, "Mr Valentine came into our dressing-room at 2.45 p.m. and told us that Mr Walker had instructed him to clamp down on the game and make sure it would be a sporting occasion."

Perhaps I should not have laughed here – big Roy became upset with me in the
Scottish Cup final later this same season

The SFA countered that by a statement from Jack Mowat where
he stressed: "It has been custom since I became chairman of the
supervisors twenty years ago to give a reminder to the match official
about the importance of the final." And Ernie Walker insisted that
he had not spoken to the referee before the game.

None of this satisfied Celtic who had ended the season empty-handed and with the added disgrace of having their skipper sent off. The board of directors supported Davie Hay and the behind-the-scenes arguments raged on until the following season when they were dealt with by the soccer bosses.

That was the general picture but there was a much more personal view of the whole affair as far as I was concerned – because I found myself being blamed for Roy Aitken being sent off. Gradually through Press reports following the match and into the next week, too, these persistent hints surfaced and all of them emanated from Parkhead, although no one was quoted.

It angered me. It hurt me too. I have never in my career tried to get a fellow professional ordered off either by feigning injury – something I hate to see in the game – or by demanding that the referee take action. That's not my way and I honestly felt that people inside and outside the game, too, would have known that. It was a slur I resented and still do.

This was an even earlier incident against Celtic in 1981. This time I was attacked at Pittodrie! (Picture: *Daily Record*)

It was a bad time for me and it affected me more than it might have done normally because it came in the midst of my transfer shambles. It was something else I could well have done without. The basic truth of the whole incident was that Roy should have known that he was going to get it in the neck for his reckless challenge on Mark McGhee in the thirty-eighth minute of that match. It had been spelled out to all of us by the referee before the game what would happen to anyone who was guilty of violent play. Whether the referee acted as he did because of the SFA instructions, is something that only he knows. But every player on the field knew that this game was to be refereed more strictly than normal.

A few weeks earlier Roy had made a similar challenge on Mark in the Premier League clash at Celtic Park. He had just brought him down when he was going through on goal. This time they clashed in midfield and Mark was sent sprawling. As soon as it happened I felt absolutely certain that the referee would take serious action against the Celtic captain. The message from Mr Valentine in the dressing-room had been very clear. I'm sure that even Roy himself must have realised that he was in trouble when he made the crude and clumsy challenge which brought the red card. There was every chance whenever he committed himself that he would be heading for a bath a little bit earlier than any of the rest of us.

That's why it hurt even more when I began to be blamed. I did not even speak to the referee following the incident, as anyone who wants to look at a video of that final will see. In fact I was late in getting over to the scene of the foul. I think that big Doug Rougvie was the first of our players to get there. I was among the last because I had been at the other side of the field when it happened. When I did arrive there was quite a stramash in progress and it was getting out of hand. But, of course, no one is ever going to pick on someone as formidable as Doug Rougvie so little old me became a handy target for abuse. But I said nothing to the referee and I did nothing which would have got Roy sent off. In any case, the referee did not require any advice on how to handle the matter. He had been given all the advice he needed from the SFA before the game!

That was the major influence, that was the most telling factor and it disappointed me that Roy and others at Parkhead did not realise that. They should have done so – and, if they had, it would have helped me avoid some pretty nasty allegations.

The strange thing was that on international trips Roy and I were often room mates. We usually ended up together when we were with Scotland and I felt genuinely sorry that he should have been sent off, particularly in a Cup final. But it was not of my doing. It was down to his own tackle and to the severity of the SFA instructions which had come about because of the behaviour of the two teams in the six previous clashes that season.

Anyhow, it was a little ironic that Roy should take offence at anyone badgering a referee. He was the master of that himself when he was with Celtic. If any decision did not suit him then he was the first to complain.

But while I have done my share of moaning at refs too, I have never done anything to get an opponent ordered off. I was hurt that people might believe that – and even more hurt that fellow professionals should suggest that it was the kind of action I could be capable of.

Eventually the whole business was forgotten and I am sure now that Roy realises that I had nothing to do with his ordering off. It's

Happy families! As I said, we all grew up together at Aberdeen and family friendships were forged there. Here's Mark McGhee and his wife Jackie along with Lesley and myself and the children

funny how things change in the game because the main protagonists that afternoon, Roy and Mark McGhee, became great buddies when Mark went to Celtic after his spell with Hamburg. They even finished up playing for a season together at Newcastle. I was with Roy after that on Scotland trips and even at the World Cup in Mexico and it all settled down. But, at the time, it was yet another reason for leaving Aberdeen and just getting away from the pressures of the Premier League.

Yet it should not have been that way. It should have been a day of celebrations. A day when we could toast another League and Cup double.

The celebrations we did have at St Andrews that night were clouded by the Aitken row and by the fact that the Aberdeen team was about to break up. They were also tinged with more than a little relief because we had struggled to beat the ten remaining Celtic players even though we were already a goal ahead when Roy was sent off.

The bother apart, it had been a good day for me because I was involved in that first goal and then, again, in the extra time winner when it arrived. We took the lead in twenty-eight minutes when I took a corner which Alex McLeish headed down towards Eric Black who hooked the ball past Pat Bonner. Celtic players appealed for offside but the linesman kept his flag down.

Then after Roy went off Murdo Macleod went to the centre of their defence and they powered foward looking for an equaliser. It came for them five minutes from the end when Paul McStay scored a marvellous goal. That thrust the final into extra time and while we were the stronger side – the extra man we had made sure of that – we managed just the one goal. But that was all we needed and, once more, I was involved. Our substitute Dougie Bell hammered a ball against the post and it broke out to me. I crossed and Mark McGhee was at the far post to finish off the move. The Scottish Cup was bound for Pittodrie after just eight minutes of that extra half-hour period.

Fifty-nine thousand people were at that game and they did not know of the backstage drama involved with both myself and Mark McGhee, also now determined to leave the club. The day after the final Mark announced that he would be joining Hamburg in the West German Bundesliga, the team we had defeated in the Super Cup over two legs. Mark had impressed their general manager, the former West German midfield ace Gunter Netzer, and he swooped knowing that Mark was out of contract.

Everything went through smoothly and quickly and I envied Mark that. I was still caught up in a horrific transfer tangle myself but I knew that I had to leave and that the incidents during and after the final had simply confirmed my determination to move.

Doug Rougvie was to move to Chelsea too. The team which had brought Aberdeen so much glory was now beginning to break up. They would have more success – but not at the level we had known in our best days. In an amazing four-year spell after Alex Ferguson took over from Billy McNeill as the manager of the club, we won two Premier League titles, three Scottish Cups, the European Cup Winners' Cup and the European Super Cup. There was a good blend in that team. We had our share of hard players and we had skilful players. We had good defenders and we had lads up front who could get us goals. It was a team which just seemed to come right for this marvellous spell at the start of the Eighties. It was a time when we seemed to dominate the game in Scotland and were even able to impose ourselves on Europe. It was a wonderful time for all of us, enhanced by the fact that so many of us had grown up together at Pittodrie. It was like one big happy family until the time arrived for some of us to leave.

I still look back at those years with really fond memories and a sense of wonder at what we did. I mean, we achieved so much more at Aberdeen than I was ever able to achieve at Old Trafford. Yet there were times in my spell with Manchester United where you were looking at a club with FIFTEEN current international players on their books. I can remember one week when all fifteen players were away from Old Trafford, off to play for their various countries and yet when we were together at club level we could not win the prize the fans most wanted – the English First Division Championship.

And, yet, my days at Aberdeen had begun badly after Billy McNeill bought me from Dundee. I had lost my way at Dens Park after being made club captain by the then manager Tommy Gemmell. I was learning too many bad habits at Dens. When the chance came to go to Aberdeen I jumped at it. It was the best decision I ever made. I still owe Billy McNeill for rescuing me from there and from all the problems which were hitting me. Dundee was a club going nowhere with all kinds of worries both on and off the field. There was a bunch of players there, at that time, who were, to say the least, unprofessional. You used to be able to smell the bevvy off the players' breath in the dressing-room on a Saturday before a game. It

Happy times at Pittodrie. Here I am jumping for joy at the prospect of taking on Bayern Munich in 1983. (Picture: Daily Record)

was a nightmare time and Dundee have never really recovered from the mistake they made back then when they did not appoint Jim McLean as manager.

I had signed for them as a youngster, when John Prentice was the team boss. Those were the best of times. The club was well run and the players were well coached under Jim McLean. There was a real professionalism about the whole place. Jim McLean was the right-hand man to the manager. As a youngster I was impressed by the set-up and by the work which was done at training sessions. But the turning point for all of us – and especially for the club – came when John Prentice left and the directors decided against making Jim McLean the new manager. He went across the street to Tannadice first as coach and then as manager and suddenly the two clubs were transformed. As Dundee sank lower and lower, United went on to the kind of success they had never known in all their long history. Jim McLean has proved himself one of the best and shrewdest coaches in the business but it has all been at a terrible cost to Dundee, the club who did not want him.

After he left the discipline soon became almost non-existent. There were good players there and good professionals too, and players whom I looked up to and respected. But they had to try to cope with the others who came into the club, who dragged it down and who quite simply couldn't care less. These were the players who were holding the rest back. They had no interest in the club and their fitness levels were dreadful because they didn't train during the week. They had no respect for themselves and none for the rest of us either. It's frightening to think of what would have happened to me if I had not got away from that atmosphere. I would never have made it. I'm sure of that in my own mind. I had a vision of myself ending up playing for Arbroath or Brechin or Forfar, one of the small clubs in the Dundee area, and just fading off the scene. One thing is sure – I was not going to make a career in football for myself if I stayed with Dundee.

I knew then that my only chance was to get away, get to a fresh club and make a fresh start and just when I felt no club was going to come in Aberdeen arrived on the scene and I got the chance I needed, though it took me some time to establish myself up at Pittodrie too.

It's amazing how much luck can play a part in all our lives. That transfer came about because of one game, more or less. It was a

Honing those ball skills with Aberdeen. (Picture: *Daily Record*)

League Cup-tie and we lost disastrously against Queen of the South at Palmerston. We had drawn 0-0 in the first leg at Dens Park and then travelled to Dumfries for the return. We crashed out of the tournament in a six-goal defeat but the Queens' manager Mike Jackson thought enough of my individual performance to recommend me to Big Billy. Mike was one of Billy's closest friends in football – he still is, I guess – and they had played together as youngsters at Celtic Park back in the days of the Kelly Kids. Their friendship lasted through the years, and as far as I was concerned that was the clincher for the rest of my career. When Mike Jackson told Billy that I refused to give in that night, that I didn't let my head go down, that I kept working and fighting and trying to get the team going again and that I was worth a gamble, Billy listened to the advice. He bought me and the rest is history – or almost.

To start with I could not get a game with Aberdeen and Billy must have been wondering if his pal's advice had been good. I was being jeered at by the fans. There were times when they were laughing at me. That's how badly I was playing. I was just a figure of fun and I couldn't fight my way into the side.

It was so bad at times that I thought I might have to move on again. I began to worry about my mortgage, about the future, and about the effect that my on-field worries would have on the rest of my life. I was only recently married and here I was with all these traumas when I should have been carving out a new beginning for myself. It was a bad time and I'm afraid that I worried myself sick over the whole thing.

I had a great relationship with the Dons fans

I could not blame anyone else for the position I found myself in. I couldn't blame the management team of Billy McNeill and John Clark for instance. It was not their fault. They had put their reputations on the line when they bought me and now here I was letting them down. It was all down to me and the rubbish I was playing. When it came to the end of the season I could not even force my way into the Aberdeen side which lost that day to Rangers. The next season Alex Ferguson arrived and I began to establish myself, but it had been an awful opening season.

Then after that it all came together and I wondered sometimes, "How did this all happen?" We never analysed it at all. There was a sense of innocence about us all back then. We just went out and played. The camaraderie was marvellous and suddenly after that first championship win it all seemed to happen. That's when I stopped worrying about whether or not I would have a career in football!

Backstage at the World Cup

IT MAY BE SOMETHING IN THE SCOTTISH MAKE UP, A natural impatience or simply a need to be constantly on the go, but when it comes to World Cups, we are well behind other countries as far as a boredom threshold is concerned.

The Italians and the West Germans, the Brazilians and the Argentinians, and all the other successful countries seem much more able to adapt to the long periods of inactivity which are a part of the tournament.

Behind the razzle dazzle, away from the circus atmosphere, light miles from the glamour and the drama which surround the games are long, long hours and dull, dull days when nothing seems to be happening. For myself all those days spent in hotels far away from the football occasions spring into my mind almost as quickly as the memories of the matches we played in.

I can remember in Spain for the Finals in 1982, the first of the two tournaments I took part in, and we stayed in Sotogrande, well down the coast from Malaga where we played two of our games. And while the facilities were superb we still had this long, long bus journey to the matches against New Zealand and Russia . . . miles and miles up one of the worst stretches of road in Europe. That stretch which carries you along the Costa del Sol is known as a killer road in Spain, and there we were at the wrong end of it as far as our matches were concerned.

I don't know how that happened. We had been at the Finals in 1974 and 1978 and we should have been able to learn from past experience.

Instead we discovered that the New Zealanders, the new boys in the tournament, the little country who had never qualified before, had a marvellous hotel much, much closer to Malaga than we were. And the Russians, too, were staying far closer to the match centre of Malaga than we were. It didn't make much sense as far as I could see.

Of course, it was even worse for me. I spent most of my time in Sotogrande sitting in a darkened room on my own. I cannot take the sun and Jock Stein was so determined that I would not suffer one bit from heat stroke that he went around the place watching me like a hawk. Any time I stayed out for more than twenty minutes or so the Big Man would be there ordering me indoors. The most exciting thing that would happen after that was when Willie Miller came into the room after his spell in the sun. Then, instead of sitting there with nothing to do, I could sit and watch Willie sleeping. That was a high spot of the afternoon and, believe me, it was no fun. The monotony was broken only by the games. Maybe if I was going to a World Cup at the age I am now I would be able to handle it better. But in Spain in 1982 and then four years later in Mexico I found it hard just to sit around like that. It's alien to our nature to be doing nothing. We are an aggressive, get up and go nation. Even on the field we are like that. You'll see the Italians or the Germans go a goal up in an important game and while they will be dominating the match they won't take chances. They'll push the ball around, let defenders pass it along the back amongst themselves and just stroll until they see an opening. We go one ahead and we are looking for one more. It's a cavalry charge forward, trying to win the game out of the park. It doesn't always work out – but it's fun while it lasts. For the players and for the fans.

It is just not a part of our national make up to be as patient as other countries so obviously are. So, while I loved playing in Spain and matching myself against some of the world's top players, the gaps between the games took their mental toll. You watched a few videos and you had your meals and you trained. Then you trained and you had your meals and you watched a few videos. Exciting stuff, isn't it?

That side of it, backstage if you like, is far removed from what the fans see. They become a part of the event on almost a daily basis. They meet the locals and they mix with the opposing fans and the time between games flies by for them. Our supporters have been magnificent and I think they have added their own dash of colour and humour to the World Cup Finals they have attended. Who can forget the carnival in Seville when the Tartan Army met up with the Brazilians? It was what the World Cup should be all about. No nastiness. No fighting. No rows. Just two sets of fans enjoying the match and our lot, even though we lost 4-1, just happy that we had been there and played against the Brazilians, a country whose footballing traditions of attacking, entertaining play, lie so close to our own view of the game.

I know that most of them would give their right arms to be able to play for Scotland and I'm not trying to bitch about things too much. I'm just pointing out some of the things which have been wrong in our preparations in the past and also emphasise that our own failings don't help in a long drawn out competition. A bunch of impatient Scots footballers cooped up together for two or three weeks in surroundings they don't like isn't any fun. But if I felt upset in Sotogrande, four years later I was wishing I could get back there instead of the hotel we used in Mexico.

For some reason the SFA had decided to stay in Mexico City – or close to Mexico City – because we played two of our games there in the slums of Neza. The West Germans stayed in Queretaro because, as seeds in the group, all their matches were played there. The Danes also stayed there although their match schedule was the same as we had. It was their first time in the Finals, but they had learned

Even before an international there's time for a laugh. Here at Hampden I share a joke with Aberdeen's Jim Bett with Maurice Malpas listening in

quickly – Mexico City and its surroundings were to be avoided at all costs. It was a message which we may have been given but no one paid any attention to it.

There had been problems for Scotland, of course, because of the tragic death of Jock Stein in Cardiff on the night we clinched a play-off spot against Australia. Alex Ferguson took over as part-time boss, still carrying on as manager of Aberdeen, but also handling the national side. It was impossible for Alex to travel to Mexico to make arrangements and so he went along with what had been arranged for him and the players by the SFA. It turned out badly. Not to put too fine a point on it, the hotel was a disaster.

The rooms were small and seemed to be carved out of stone to give a 'natural' effect. To me it was like living in a cave. Honestly, I felt like a bear cub sitting in a cave waiting for someone to come along and toss me a few scraps of meat. Except I would not have been allowed to eat the meat because most of the grub was so bad. And, while we were out of the city by quite a distance, the pollution was still dreadful. I wasn't going to have to worry about sun stroke there – you didn't see much of the sun because of the pall of smoke which hung over the whole area. It was the most desolate spot I have known for any team to stay for any length of time.

I suppose, too, there was a culture shock for all of us because for that World Cup we were away from home even longer than usual because of the various problems which exist for players in Mexico. Most of the problems stemmed from the altitude and so we spent some time getting acclimatised in Santa Fe which was at the same altitude as Mexico City. This allowed the medical staff to monitor all of us and check in case anyone was adversely affected. So we spent two weeks there training and playing in bounce games against the Northern Ireland side who were in Albuquerque. After that, we came down to normal altitude to Los Angeles to play again there, because medical reports suggested that we should have a spell back at sea level before going into Mexico itself. All of that seemed to work OK and I was never worried by the altitude. Only the variation in the flight of the ball offered me any bother at all on that front.

But, after the States, Mexico was a nightmare. From being able to eat anything you wanted and being able to relax in front of the television in your room or even go out into Santa Fe, we now found ourselves under armed guard in this grim, little hotel near the Mexican Pyramids. That was the sole attraction of the area and I think if you know footballers at all then you'll realise that sightseeing at the Aztec Pyramids isn't high on our list of priorities. Even if it had been, it would have occupied only an hour or so – hardly enough to compensate for the time we had to spend cooped up. There was nothing for us to do. There were a few souvenir stalls around the Pyramids selling junk, and that was the lot. No television. A handful of videos you were soon fed up watching. A table-tennis room. Oh, and the weather was just as good. You could set your watch by the thunderstorms and torrential rain which came every afternoon.

Acapulco this was not! In fact I have never been able to figure out why the SFA chose this hotel. They claimed that they were first on the spot and this was where other countries had wanted to stay. I just wish they had been beaten to the booking. We would have been better off living in tents. The West Germans and the Danes had it right, as we discovered when we moved up to Queretaro to play the match against the Germans. We were away from the pollution, there was fresh air to breathe, and the hotel we were in was perfect – it was the one which the Danes were using as their HQ. How I envied them. They had made the right decision – stay out of Mexico City until you had to go in. They moved down for their games and then whenever it was physically possible raced back to their own hotel.

OK, we were not in the city itself but where we were was hardly the classiest suburb. On the way out of the capital to where we were based you passed shanty town after shanty town where people were living in real poverty. It broke my heart to see them.

When we were allowed into the city for one day's shopping, just to help break the boredom, we could not move for beggars. We had these gangs of youngsters just following us, looking for any pesos we might have. Or, even better, any US dollars we might have. By the time I walked along just one street I had virtually emptied my pockets and the rest of the lads were the same. You felt awful when you came face to face with the poverty these people accept as a normal part of their everyday life.

All of that simply helped put me on another downer. Outside the hotel we found conditions we would never have seen at home. I felt guilty that we were there to play football in marvellous, newly constructed stadiums when the people were so abjectly poor. And I felt guilty that we should be moaning about hotels and food when these ordinary Mexicans looked as if they were starving, and were probably

Soon Gavin and Craig will be fighting over these jerseys – but not yet. These are just some of the jerseys I have collected over the years

staying in the cardboard and corrugated-iron shanties we could see lining the roads out of the capital city.

But, then, you had to detach yourself from that and remember that you were there to do a job. You had to get on with it. The problem was that the conditions in the hotel were so bad that few of us were happy. And if players are not happy with their living conditions then they won't give their best when they go on to the field. There will be plenty of people who disagree with me, but I honestly believe that footballers must have the very best of facilities. That is the only way if you are going to be asked to perform at the peak of your ability. At club level with the three major sides I have played for, I have always found that the very best of hotels and training facilities were provided for the players. At Aberdeen and Manchester and at Leeds it has always been that way; even when we were playing in some of the worst countries in Eastern Europe it was made as comfortable as possible for us and the best of food was brought in on the charter plane we always used.

The conditions we had to contend with in Mexico would not have been tolerated by Alex Ferguson for Aberdeen. Knowing him, he would have led us out of the place after just one look around. We felt let down by the planning and all of us knew that the other countries we were playing against were living in better conditions than we were. That was wrong.

As well as all of those problems we had the medical worries. I'm still amazed that all of us survived that World Cup. You had to be careful about what you were eating – everything was vetted for us. And you had to make sure that you used bottled water all the time, even for cleaning your teeth. Then you had to take various tablets every day to ward off illnesses such as malaria. It was more like a medical convention than a football World Cup. Our whole stay there, apart from the few days when we saw the sun at Queretaro, was a nightmare.

I've always maintained that the football is the one good thing about the tournament, the actual playing of the games, and that was more true in Mexico than it was in Spain. In fact, after the games there the next most exciting thing was brushing your teeth!

I honestly believe that the SFA should have looked after the players much better than they did in these two tournaments I took part in. I was not in Italy but from what the players have told me it was much better. The hotels were good, the food was good, and the boredom factor was reduced. Maybe the lessons had been learned. I would like to think so because after FOUR appearances in the Finals they should have been able to get things right when they got to Italy in 1990.

Oh, and just as a P.S. to this chapter. I found myself in a room on my own at the Pyramids, and right next to me was the manager, Alex Ferguson. So I had the added bonus of lying there wide awake night after night, listening to that nervous cough he has when he is under pressure. That just made the trip for me . . .

And then there were the games!

Then comes the Action!

IT HAS BEEN FRUSTRATING FOR SCOTLAND ON EVERY occasion they have qualified for the final stages of the World Cup. After five appearances, we have still to reach the second stage.

My first time at the Finals in 1982 was no exception when we were drawn against Brazil, Russia and New Zealand. Just as on the two previous occasions – in West Germany and in Argentina – we failed on goal difference. We played well in those three games, though. Even when we were thumped 4-1 by Brazil we had the consolation of knowing that Dave Narey had scored a spectacular opener. Mind you, some of us thought it might have been better if big Dave had not scored that goal because it just seemed to upset the Brazilians a little bit. They hit back and when that team hit back there was no stopping them. You are looking at Falcao and Cerezo and Zico and Junior, and I suppose they were always going to be too good for us. But that was acceptable. The team boss then, the late Jock Stein, had always reckoned that the last game against Russia would hold the key to qualification. He was right. But the Soviet stars were the men who turned that key and opened the door to the second round of matches for themselves.

The Russians were a powerful side and we matched them until a crazy mistake in our defence allowed them in for one of the goals. Two of the most reliable players in our team, Willie Miller and Alan Hansen, went for the same ball. They collided, the ball broke loose and the Russians went 2-1 in front. Graeme Souness scored a great goal to level the scores before the end but it was not enough. The Russians had the better goal difference, and through they went.

No one could have legislated for that mistake. You had Willie, the Mr Consistency of the Aberdeen team, and Alan, the most influential figure in the Liverpool defence, and they made a hash of things. It should never have happened and the two players know that for themselves. It would never have happened again. But it was just another instance of our cruel World Cup luck that night in Malaga.

I still look back and wonder at it. As far as I was concerned, you could not get two better defenders in Europe. Willie is the player I would pick second in any team of greats I could name – and the only player ahead of him would be Kenny Dalglish. Quite simply, Kenny was the most gifted Scottish player of his generation, but I'd place Willie next even though he came nowhere near Kenny's skills.

Willie had other attributes. For my money he was, at one stage in his career, the best penalty-box defender in the world. He was not the quickest but he could size up situations very, very quickly and make his move to nip any attacks in the bud before they became too dangerous. He was a tremendous tackler and his timing was immaculate. He was often underestimated by foreign teams who came to play us but never by any of the Aberdeen team we played in together. He also had marvellous leadership qualities, which I can't stress enough.

Then you had Alan – our answer to the skilled defenders they have on the Continent. Alan had that kind of class, the kind that Beckenbauer and Augenthaler had. If he had been born in West

Willie Miller, "the best penalty-box defender in the world", pictured here in action against Hearts' Dave McPherson

Germany he would have had well over a hundred caps. Instead he had to settle for less than thirty with Scotland. That was a national disgrace!

When you have two players of that calibre, the last thing you expect is for a mistake to be made. Sadly, though, that's what happened. We could not believe our eyes. Neither could the Russians. That goal is what eventually pushed us out with the Russians and ourselves each gathering three points, but with them having a two-goal advantage over us.

It was a major disappointment because we thought we would be able to reach the next stage, and we wanted to do it so much for all those thousands of fans who seemed to have taken over the Costa del Sol for the two weeks we were there. We would make that long, long drive up to Malaga and they would be lining the route, sitting in the bars and restaurants waving their flags and their banners. They help to make these World Cup trips memorable for all of us. They add colour to the whole event and they lift us in games, they really do.

Even on the ill-fated trip to Mexico they were over there in their thousands, willing us to the victories they wanted so badly. Unfortunately it was not to be. And that time I felt we did not give a good account of ourselves. We might have done better, even though we were in a section which the Mexican hosts had dubbed the 'Group of Death'. West Germany were there – and they went on to be runners-up to Argentina. Uruguay were there – another country with a noted World Cup pedigree. And as the unseeded team Denmark were also in that group. Unseeded! It was a bit of a joke that one. The Danes were rated one of the most powerful nations in Europe at that time and two years before had been semi-finalists in the European Championships which took place in France. They had gifted players, a talented West German manager in Sepp Piontek, and a marvellous track record over the previous four seasons.

But because of the vagaries of World Cup seeding, the fact that the Danes had not played in the Finals before meant that they were placed in the group of countries rated lowest among the twenty-four countries which had reached Mexico. They were alongside the South Koreans, Iraq and Canada – and it was our luck that we had to play them in our opening game.

They had so many top players – the veteran skipper Morton Olsen, Soren Lerby, Jan Molby, Jesper Olsen, and up front the twin strikers, Preben Elkjaer and Michael Laudrup. They had a wonderful team and yet they managed to beat us just 1-0 with a freak goal from Elkjaer in the second half. He went for the ball and it struck his knee and went past Jim Leighton. Until then we had matched them well, and you are talking about a team here who were going to hammer six goals past Uruguay in their next match and then beat the eventual winners, West Germany, 2-0 in the final group clash.

We had our own chances, too. One came late in the game when Charlie Nicholas was going through on goal and was hacked down by their midfield player, Claus Berggren. It was a shocking professional foul and the Danish player was later to admit that to the world's Press. He said quite cynically, "I am a professional and I had to stop the Scotland player, Nicholas, from scoring. I would do the same again." He was booked but Charlie limped off with around ten minutes to go, and was also missing from our next match against West Germany. In fact, he only made it as a substitute against the Uruguayans, and was not one hundred per cent fit for that appearance.

Ironically, if FIFA had tightened up their disciplinary code then the Danish player Berggren would have been automatically red-carded. Today, under the new code, there is no doubt that he would have been OFF. That might just have given us the breakthrough we needed to get a result.

The planning had been good for the game. Alex Ferguson and Walter Smith had worked out exactly how they would play, and we possibly deserved a little more than that single point we got. But worse was to come. Much, much worse.

We went in against the West Germans next, and here we took the lead when I scored the first goal of the game in twenty minutes. Our lead didn't last long – within four minutes Voeller had equalised for them. Then right at the start of the second half Allofs pushed them in front after our defence found themselves in a bit of a tangle. But no excuses this time. They were better than we were, just as the Brazilians had been in Seville four years ealier.

There are times in football when you just have to own up and accept that you have to take second place. The West Germans had a star-studded squad – Brieghel and Foerster and Brehme and Matthaus and Allofs and Voeller and Magath and Rummenigge. Little wonder they reached the Final and pushed Maradona and Co so close in the Aztec Stadium.

So, there we were, two games played and two defeats, and yet, amazingly, because of the structure of the tournament we still had an

Here I was in the hot seat in Mexico before the match against Denmark.
(Picture: *Daily Record*)

opportunity to qualify. When we looked at our own section and at the other five we knew that a win against Uruguay would still carry us into the knock-out stages.

The South Americans, though, were in a better position than we were. Although they had crashed to a shattering 6-1 defeat from the Danes, they had drawn their first group game against the Germans. A draw against us would be enough to give them one of the places in the last sixteen. As that fact seeped through and was digested by the watching football world, it became more and more clear that we were going to find it very difficult against them. The word coming out of their training camp was all about how they feared our physical game, and yet there had already been signs of their violence in the two matches they had played. Their propaganda seemed to be setting the stage for trouble and they were trying to cast themselves in the role of victims. Scotland, naturally, were the villains. We were going to be the bad guys. The build up was not good and FIFA, the world soccer bosses, were monitoring the situation as countdown came nearer and nearer.

We all had an idea of what to expect. We had seen the South Americans in action on the box. I exempt the Brazilians from this, but the Argentinians and the Uruguayans had deserved reputations for making trouble, and for the kind of cynical ruthlessness which our players and, for that part, most Europeans cannot accept. They will do things on the field which would never cross the minds of any player in British football. They will spit, they will scratch, they will pull your hair and they will kick you when the ball is nowhere near, and then if you even look at them, they'll drop down as if they have been pole-axed, looking to the referee to send you off. They will do anything to achieve victory and they see nothing wrong in that warped and wicked philosophy. We got all of that and more in Neza that day, and it sickened me and all the rest of us.

That June day brought ninety minutes of hell for all of us. From the first minute of the game we knew what we were in for – though, I suppose, we had suspected beforehand what was going to happen. I knew that I was going to be one of the targets for their hatchet men, but I can't say that this worried me too much. When you are my size and my type of player, you become used to having special attention paid to you by opposing defenders. It's something you learn to live with as long as you feel that you will get protection from the referee. I expected to take a bit of a kicking. I wasn't disappointed.

In that opening minute I was hacked down by Jose Batista and the French referee, Joel Quiniou, immediately brought out the red card, showed it emphatically to the Uruguayan player and ordered him off. It was an early warning for the South Americans – the earliest possible – but in some ways it backfired.

It seemed to increase their resentment, made them more determined to stop us at all costs, and it was clear to everyone at the game that if the referee sent off another of their players then there would be a riot. He had a hard enough job getting Batista off and then re-starting the game. Any further attempts to control them would have caused mayhem.

The game was a powder keg waiting to explode, for everyone except the Uruguayan players, their manager and backroom staff. For them this was a matter of national pride. The world was ranged against Uruguay and they had to show the people back home that no matter what was needed from them, they would qualify. Yes, it was turned round that way. They saw nothing wrong in what they did. They were the victims, poor innocent victims of a FIFA plot to keep them out of the last sixteen.

I can't remember too many of the details of the game, of the actual football played – not that there was much of that allowed. We missed an early chance when Steve Nicol shot over the bar. That might have made a difference, but I don't know. They were absolutely determined that we would not succeed and we could do very little about it.

We were quite literally afraid to do anything. One of our greatest assets is always our national fervour. The passion we have for the game and the natural aggression we show on the park carries us through, at times, against opposition which may be much more highly talented. Other teams can be more sophisticated. Other teams can be better technically. Other teams can be more disciplined and more organised . . . but Scottish teams can still beat them. That, however, was not on the cards against the South Americans. We were too frightened to give in to our natural instincts and have a real go in the game. Not frightened of being kicked or even of being injured. We expected that. But frightened that if we fought fire with fire there would be a riot.

If just one of us retaliated then there would have been one of those huge on-field brawls where anything might have happened. If one of our players had resorted to the type of tackle which hammered me down in the first minute of the game, then the same would have happened. They were out for blood. They would have welcomed us losing our tempers. They would have been happy to draw us into violence, and then they would have found it easier to lay the blame at our door. For our part we had been warned by Alex Ferguson to walk away from trouble and I think we knew ourselves that one wrong move could have brought a riot. Then we would have been the country in disgrace. It was like playing a football match in a mine-field where one wrong step was going to finish everything.

I had come up against cynical players before – most of us had. At various times in European matches you face people who want to win at all costs. Even at home you can occasionally find that, though nothing to the extent you find abroad. This, though, was beyond anything we had ever been asked to combat. I mean, you can expect problems any time you come up against a Latin country because it brings you a clash of soccer cultures. They don't like the physical approach of the British and we hate things that they do. Spitting, for instance, is an action which angers everyone I know in this country. They will do that without compunction and it is no big deal to them. Similarly, where our players will accept a strong but fair tackle, they won't. So there are always liable to be niggles, or worse, major clashes. Yet against Brazil in Spain there had been none of that. This time there was an ugly backdrop to the game. We were seeing the unacceptable face of South American soccer.

We were being spat on.

We were being punched when the ball was maybe fifty yards away.

We were victims of vicious forearm smashes across the face when the referee and linesmen were not looking.

We were having our hair pulled by them when they came to help us up after savagely hacking us down in a tackle.

We were being punched in the back when we waited for a throw in to be taken.

We were watching them drop like ninepins at the slightest touch to allow their army of medical men to come on to the field and waste time.

It was sickening. I can remember thinking at one stage that if you had to sink as low as this to find success in a World Cup, then it was just not worth it.

While we cared deeply about the image of our country and the image of football, they didn't give that a thought. Or not in the way we did. While we worried quite genuinely about the possibility of a riot, they couldn't have cared less. In fact, if our fans had come on – and they would have been sorely tempted if a battle on the pitch had taken place between the two teams – they might even have welcomed that. All these situations kept careering through our minds as we tried to get on with the game, tried our best to get the result we wanted. I even thought that it was possible people could die in that stadium that day. If there had been a crowd break-in and the Mexican police had used their anti-riot powers, who is to say what might have happened? That would have been a terrible thing to have on your conscience. Throughout the ninety minutes we were always skirting close to that possibility. All for a game of football.

So we did not retaliate. We knew that we would be punched when the referee had his back turned to follow play and we knew that they would have the blow timed to perfection. They seemed able to strike when even the linesmen were looking in the other direction. You were out there and you would see a shadow or sense that someone was coming up behind you and then – WHACK! You braced yourself for the punch and you then counted to ten to keep your temper – and all the time you were doing that you knew that it would happen again. And again. And again. Nothing was going to stop it. Nothing but the final whistle would end the madness. When that came it was a blessed relief, even though we had failed to qualify. We left Mexico the next day with just a single point – but with some dignity still intact. And the Uruguayans marched on.

They were hammered by the World Cup Disciplinary Committee at a specially convened meeting. The committee fined the Uruguayans £7,000, and warned that any repeat of their hooligan behaviour would see them kicked out of the competition. Their coach, Omar Borras, was banned from the dug-out in the next game which was to be against Argentina. FIFA warned that they would not accept any further 'unruly conduct' from him. A spokesman for the world bosses added: "There was ungentlemanly behaviour on the bench, though much more serious was the fact that the referee was molested. Mr Borras used uncouth language in reference to the referee afterwards." Borras had said after the game, "There was a murder on the field today and the murderer was the referee." Our own SFA secretary referred to the South Americans as the "scum of the earth". He was right and Borras was simply trying to cover for his own players' conduct.

None of the actions by FIFA helped us any. It was too late. We were flying home, while the Uruguayans were still there. They got what they wanted – that place in the last sixteen. When they were beaten in their next match, they could turn round and say that they lost to Argentina who went on to win the Jules Rimet trophy. They could also use the FIFA decision as an excuse to prove to the people back home that they had been cheated. They handed out propaganda that it was all a FIFA plot, that the Brazilians feared them, that the President of FIFA, Joao Havelange, was a Brazilian and therefore the verdict against them was rigged. I'm quite sure that by the time they repeated that nonsense often enough they believed it. The truth was far, far different.

They had no conception of fair-play that day. They had been told that they had to qualify. They had been told that they could not fail their nation. They had been told that everyone was against them, and they believed all of that. We were sitting ducks.

And yet as we drove away from the stadium, that magnificent new stadium which stood out of its slum surroundings like some kind of obscenity, I found myself able to understand them. Here we were passing through the kind of streets that so many of the South American footballers grow up in. Dead dogs were lying in the road. People were living in cardboard houses. The children were in rags, and most of them looked as if they had not had a decent meal in days. Yet they had this stadium which had cost so many millions of pounds and they had seen people from all corners of the globe come to watch the football there, and be upset by the squalor which surrounded it.

I realised then that the Uruguayans, who had just used every dirty trick in the book to beat us would do it all again as long as it meant a permanent escape from the slums. It is the old hungry fighter thing, and you can see why the Argentinians and the Uruguayans approach football with a life or death attitude. In some ways, that is what the game means to them. It is their means of survival. It has given them a new life, and probably handed whole families the lifeline they would never otherwise have reached. They can take their mothers and fathers, their brothers and sisters, away from slums like Neza. They can marry and raise a family in decent surroundings and educate their children. Even feed and clothe them . . . because they have been born with soccer skills.

That's some motivation. And sure as hell we could not match it! You see, if one of us had been sent off in a World Cup match then we would have felt that we had let everyone down. There would have been a stigma attached to the incident. That is not the way with them. If their action helped the team achieve its ambition, be it victory or be it the draw they needed against us, they would look on the red card as some badge of honour.

They know that when they spit on you they are doing something to you that you hate. Their view from then on is to keep doing it because it will affect the opposition during the game. If you're angry then you won't be as effective as a player. All of it is calculated. I don't know how they can look themselves in the mirror if they have spent ninety minutes spitting at opponents, but it does not faze them one little bit. As long as their manager is happy and they are getting some success then anything goes.

While I found some understanding of their behaviour I'm sure they would never be able to understand how we put up with all the abuse we had that day. They would not have shown the same tolerance. But we had no choice. To behave in the same way as they did would have brought riots. Worse, we would have descended to the same level as they did, and I know not a single one of us wanted to do that. In fact, I felt a profound sense of relief at the end of the game and knowing that the tournament was over for us made up part of that feeling I had. I was happy to be heading for home. Sure, we felt ill-done by and I'm sure that most countries who remained in Mexico would rather that we had stayed than the Uruguayans. But, at the time, I was sickened by it all.

I had never experienced anything as bad as that before and I'm happy to say I have never come up against it since. I doubt if any of the players who played that day would want to go through it all again. Most of us were just happy to get out of Mexico and away from football for a spell, to get the bad taste out of our mouths.

Sometimes I feel I have never managed to do that because the videos of these games are still in the house. I have never watched a single minute of them. Normally I like to see the games again – that's why I have videos made – but these three have never been taken out of their boxes. It's a nasty episode that I would rather not be reminded of. Football is not worth all that ugliness. Pele always called it the beautiful game and the Uruguayans should try to remember that and live up to it.

Of course, even in defeat there just had to be controversy and argument surrounding our exit. It wouldn't be the same if we were a happy, settled group of players. There has just got to be something, whether it is right or not. The slightest problem is magnified and this time it was the axing of the Scotland captain Graeme Souness for that last match against the South Americans. Since it happened, Alex Ferguson has gone on record as saying that it might have been a mistake to leave out a player of his experience. Whether right or wrong, it was a brave decision that Alex made. He must have known the repercussions and criticisms there would be and yet he did what he thought was right.

Knowing him as well as I do, I'd say that it was the type of thing only he would do. If he reckoned that the change had to be made then he would do it and if he was wrong then he would take the flak. More often than not, though, in my experience he was right.

Funnily enough, I did not realise what had happened when the team was read out. It's always the same. You sit there among the rest of the lads and you are waiting to see if your own name is there. Once you hear that everything else is a kind of blur. It is only later that you pick up on the whole team and you realise that someone has been dropped, or the team has been changed for tactical reasons or whatever. So when the team was announced it was not as if a bombshell had hit me – I didn't notice until later.

Now, looking back, I agree with Alex Ferguson that it was probably wrong to leave him out completely. Graeme had all that experience in Italy which would have helped us so much when they were down to ten men. After all, Graeme was one of the best players around at that time. Not just in Britain, but in Europe he was recognised as a great midfield man. So when he was left out – and the Press did not know until just before kick-off – it was a shock. It was a surprise to the players too, once we sat down and digested the team announcement. We found it hard to grasp that the captain had been dropped. I think Graeme was as shocked as anyone. Yet there had been signs that Graeme was tired. He had suffered weight-loss and severe dehydration like so many of us during the two earlier games. After the match against the Germans he had looked scarcely able to walk. All of us were suffering, and some were getting back to fitness quicker than others. Graeme had extra pressures on his shoulders, too, of course.

A couple of months previously he had been appointed player-manager of Rangers, and he was going home to start the job of re-fashioning the Ibrox team. It was another burden for the guy to

Graeme Souness: it was probably wrong to leave him out against the Uruguayans

carry, another off-field pressure which could have been affecting him. He had looked in the game against West Germany as if he was playing his last game of the season. He looked really drained, and perhaps that was why Alex made his decision. I don't know. No one but Alex does. In those circumstances you have to try to understand the manager's situation and while Graeme must have been angry at the time I'm sure that now that he is on the other side of the fence

115

as a manager himself he realises that harsh decisions – even cruel ones – sometimes have to be made for the team's sake. Graeme made them himself when he had to drop Terry Butcher at Rangers, for big Terry had been one of the men he had built his team around. Yet, when the time came and Graeme thought that he had to be left out then that's what happened. Terry was soon on his way back down south to join Coventry as player/boss. It happens. It's a part of the game, and even when you are the victim – and I have been – you don't hold grudges. You get on with your life and your career.

I'm sure that's what Graeme did. As for those of us who played, we had to do something the same because we had been exposed to the dark underbelly of the game, to the sickness which lurks just beneath the surface whenever you have to face the players from Uruguay or Argentina. They have skills but they waste them. Cheating takes over, and the unhappiest thing of all is that often, in football, cheats do prosper.

Across the Great Divide

PEOPLE ALWAYS LOOK FOR REASONS WHY SCOTTISH international teams can go so far in the World Cup – and then, seemingly, no further. We can reach the Finals as we have done on FIVE consecutive occasions. But once we are there, we are heading back home immediately after the first series of games. I don't know if I can explain it, but I don't think it has anything to do with the great divide which has sometimes split the Scottish camp: that gap between the home Scots and the Anglos which has existed at times, and which has brought its share of friction in the get-togethers.

Now that I have been on both sides of the split I feel qualified to talk a little bit about it. There is no doubt in my mind that there have been faults on both sides.

As a home Scot, winning my early caps for my country when Jock Stein was the manager, I used to arrive in awe of some of the Anglos. I think most of us had the feeling that they were big-timers. You arrived ready to accept that they were going to be acting superior but, looking back, I don't think too many of them did give that impression. It was as much in our minds as anything.

The divide between the two camps was fairly obvious during the period when I was one of the new kids on the block. You would walk into the dining-room of the hotel, or maybe into the lounge, and you would see the two groups – seven or eight players at one table and another seven or eight at the other and never the twain would meet. There might be the odd intruder in one of the groups. But, basically, it was a 'them and us' situation.

However there was a simple explanation for all of that, although it was not something which hit any of the home Scots at the time. These lads were playing in a different League – at that time it was a 'different League' in almost every way – and they were then travelling up to Scotland for games together. They would be on the same aeroplanes or they would be sharing cars. It was only natural that they would stick together when they arrived at the team HQ. Also when they were sitting around, or having meals, again it was natural that they would gravitate towards each other because they had things to talk about. They would be discussing what was going on in the First Division and how certain teams were playing and what had happened the last time they played against each other. Meanwhile, we would be doing the same in our own groups. That was OK, though, we didn't see anything wrong with that.

You would find also that guys from the same club would almost automatically room together. Kenny Dalglish and Graeme Souness would share rooms at home and abroad, so you didn't get the chance to mingle with them all that often.

Our problem – the home Scots, I mean – was that we had a bit of a chip on our shoulders about the big money that was being made by the lads in England. The difference in the wage structures then was immense. It has been closed somewhat as far as the major clubs in Scotland are concerned but back then, ten years or so ago, the gap was huge. We felt like second class citizens and we resented that.

I would drive to Troon or wherever we were meeting in my old Vauxhall Viva, praying that it wouldn't rain because then the car would probably break down. And I'd park it, this battered old rust-bucket, beside some of the flash cars that the English-based players had driven up in. I felt lousy. So the divide was there and the faults lay on both sides. I see that even more clearly now, having come back into the side as an 'Anglo'.

Of course the fires of resentment were stoked by the stories you would hear of Anglo players behaving badly or getting preferential treatment from the manager. Some of them were true, some were not, but the myth-making went on and I'm sure that the Anglo players also had some stories about our lot.

The worst I knew of – and this was one that was true – happened when Paul Hegarty, the Dundee United centre-half, was called into an international squad. He was brought in at the last minute, after injuries had forced other players to call off. This was his first time with the group and he was rooming with one of the Anglos. Now, without the call-offs, that might never have been the case. Still, that's the way it worked out and in the afternoon the players were sent up to their rooms to rest. They had to report downstairs at six o'clock for a team talk before the evening meal. Six o'clock came and

Resting after a kick-about in the garden with sons Gavin and Craig

The full family picture with Lesley and myself and the three children, Gavin, Gemma and Craig

the lads were assembling in the room which had been set aside for them when the manager – I think it was Jock Stein by this time – came in. He checked the numbers, found one player missing and after another check realised it was Paul Hegarty.

His room-mate, though – and he has to remain nameless – was there, bright-eyed and bushy-tailed. So Big Jock says, "Where's Paul Hegarty? Has anyone seen him?"

Now here you have a really embarrassing situation for Paul. He is a late choice, a relative newcomer to the Scotland scene, and he is the ONLY player who is missing from this team talk. Now his room-mate speaks up and says: "Yeah, I know where he is. He's still in his bed."

Jock looks at him and says: "Did you not give him a shake? Did you not waken him when you were coming downstairs?"

The answer he got was a classic. "It's not my job to waken players who sleep in."

That happened. Paul was the unfortunate victim and the legacy was a mutual distrust between the two groups of players which took a long time to go away. It was unnecessary and it was deliberate, and it should not have happened.

That was probably the worst incident I ever encountered and it was not the norm. There were differences but they were not huge. It was just that the two groups did not seem to mingle to any extent. I guess it was probably worse in other times when there were maybe more Anglos than home-based players. In my time the balance moved away from that. Jock Stein recognised the ability of the home players and not only those with the Old Firm. He saw how Aberdeen and Dundee United were performing at home and in Europe, and he began to use players from both clubs as a powerful part of his squads.

He was shrewd enough to realise that the experience we were gaining in Europe with our clubs – and the reputations we were building for ourselves on the Continent – would be of value to the team. He also followed the managerial philosophy at international level that it was a good thing to have as many players from the same clubs as possible in the team. That way club understandings could be utilised rather than simply putting out a team of strangers who had to get to know each other as well as try to combat the opposition.

Of course the Anglos had their own problems and I have found out what some of these are since making the move south of the border. There seems to be more pressure heaped on them. The fans seem to believe that because they are playing in England they won't give the same effort for their country. That's not true.

In fact when I have played since leaving Aberdeen I have felt more pressure on me to do well. I have been desperate to prove that my move south doesn't lessen any patriotism I may feel. Often you find that the lads who have to stand a lot of kidding from the English lads at their clubs all through the season want to show them what Scotland can achieve. I've felt that – and I know lots of the others have felt the same. You want to play for your country, you want to do well for your country and if you happen to be what the media describe as a 'big name Anglo' then you know that you MUST do well. If you don't, then you carry the can for whatever goes wrong. That is the other side of the coin.

You can be really buzzing at your club, there isn't a cloud on the horizon, and then you go back to play for Scotland and things go wrong. You find that the newspapers are giving you four stars out of ten and your picture appears with a big axe sticking out of your neck. The message is clear. It's awful, and it then affects your whole club situation as well. You go back and your confidence is shattered. You have to try to get that back for the next match even though you know you are being written off as an international player. Being an Anglo, your reputation at home depends on what happens that night at Hampden or wherever the game takes place. If it's abroad then the verdicts from the punters are reached from watching television.

Yet though you realise that you catch all the flak when defeats occur it still doesn't stop you turning up. I went through all of this myself when Andy Roxburgh brought me back to play against France in Paris in a World Cup game. It was a crucial tie in the Parc des Princes and the French wanted revenge against us after losing in Glasgow. I had not played in the Hampden game and I had been out of the picture for a couple of years. But Andy spoke to me and said he wanted me back in the side. He felt I could do a job and I decided to take a gamble, go to Paris and do my best. I was in my first full season at Leeds, coping with the demands of the Second Division and the dreams of promotion. But deep down I knew that I still wanted to play for Scotland, even if there was the chance of a bad match and all the recriminations that would surely follow.

Well, as you all know, we lost 3-0 that night, as the French played as well as we had done at Hampden. But I did not have a good night and my stock slumped after that defeat.

I felt a little unhappy about what had happened. I was the only player who had to play on the weekend before the game. The Scottish domestic programme had been postponed and the First Division programme in England had also been wiped out as the English squad also had an international the following midweek. But I was in the Second Division now and it was business as usual which meant we were playing West Ham at Upton Park in a crucial game. It was a match we won, and one which helped us eventually get promotion at the end of that season. I had to play. My priority in that situation had to lie with the club – but I suffered because of it. The other players had longer to prepare. They had had the benefit of a rest on the Saturday and had joined up with the squad days in front of me. Here I was – back to being a new boy after being absent for so long – trying to find my feet in a pool of players which had changed a whole lot since I had been there last. I felt a little bit of a stranger. Everyone was OK with me, the lads were fine, but somehow I just didn't feel a part of things. I'm not making any excuses here, just stating how things were on that ill-fated comeback.

I just had the feeling that I was on the outside looking in, and I don't blame anyone for that. It was as if I was a visitor rather than one of the players and I suppose that's just how I felt because this was in the middle of the qualifying games and I had not been a part of the others when the team had done so well. I also felt as if I was a little bit on trial, the ageing Second Division player trying to make a comeback. It was a funny feeling, and even though I had been playing well with Leeds and enjoying my football, I could not shake that off.

In a way it was the other side of the old Anglo question raising its head. I WAS on trial and in some people's eyes I WAS a little bit of an outsider now. The Press and the fans would judge me that way. When I had a bad game I knew I would be slaughtered. And I was.

Nothing came off for us that night, though, to be fair, the French played superbly well. This was their night and they knew that they had to have an outstanding result if they were to pip Scotland for the second qualifying place in the section. The first was certain to go to Yugoslavia while Cyprus and Norway were out of things. The French were buzzing that night and we were not given a chance to show what we could do.

It hurt me because I thought my career was over. I had already had more farewell performances than Sinatra and this one, I thought, saw the end of things. I felt, well, it was good while it lasted but after

A Scotland training session with club-mate Brian McClair.
(Picture: *Daily Record*)

forty-two caps I only wished I had given the Scottish fans better memories of how I could play. Luckily Andy came back for me during the European Championships. I'll deal with these games later.

But, at that time, I felt wounded by the criticism and realised, again, how much your reputation can sometimes depend on a single game. Just ninety minutes can destroy all you had built up throughout your career. After all, not too many fans at home would be particularly aware of how I was doing with Leeds. That was the Second Division after all. So I went back to Elland Road determined to help them get promotion, and tried not to let the Scotland experience affect my game there. Possibly because of my length of time in the game it didn't. I just buckled down and got on with things.

123

I knew, though, that if I had been younger and more vulnerable then my club form could also have been damaged. It was a bad week for me and a bad result for Scotland and I was not surprised that I was not picked again or that even when we qualified for the World Cup Finals in Italy, I scarcely rated a mention. Being chosen for these games didn't even cross my mind.

Almost more than two years had passed before I got the call from Andy again. This really did resurrect my Scotland career. Yet I have to admit that I was in two minds whether to accept it or not. I did not want to have to go through all the traumas of failure again. While I had helped Leeds get promotion and we were now going well in the First Division I remained aware of the pitfalls I faced. Another bad game and I would be written off as being too old: people would be pick, pick, picking away at any reputation I had built for myself at Leeds. I would have been dubbed a waste of time. I weighed all of that up when Andy Roxburgh spoke to me. Then I decided to take the gamble. There is a masochistic streak in all of us, I suppose. You really do want to play for Scotland no matter how many problems that can throw up. I did worry a bit about my decision but deep down I always knew that I would travel up to Glasgow for the friendly game against Russia at Ibrox. And I knew, too, that I wanted this chance to show the Tartan Army what I could do. I wanted to let them see that I was a better player than the one they had seen in Paris. I wanted to say to them: "This is me! This is how I am playing week after week with my club and I still think I'm good enough for international football and fit enough to do the job Scotland want me to do!"

This time it worked out for me and I stayed in the team. I also found myself impressed by the way Andy Roxburgh has settled into the job as international team boss. I believe he has helped in little ways to break down the barriers I was talking about at the start of this chapter. His attention to detail helps ensure that there are no cliques built up in the squad. Club-mates don't share with each other as a matter of course any longer. They are moved around and that way a better understanding grows among all of the players.

I can provide a perfect example of that. In Mexico for the World Cup in 1986, we moved away from our HQ just outside Mexico City to Queretaro to ready ourselves for our game there against West Germany. For some reason or other the rooming arrangements were altered while we were there. I had been on my own in

Another First Division clash with my old club. Here I'm trying to get clear of
Gary Pallister with Steve Bruce watching anxiously from behind

Mexico City but when we travelled for this second game of the
Finals I found myself rooming with Graeme Souness. You know,
for all the trips we had been on together, and these included the
previous World Cup Finals in Spain in 1982 that was the first time
that Graeme and I sat down, and talked about how we felt the
game should be played. I mean we REALLY talked. We were
together in the room and we had our own ideas. We knocked them
back and forward between us and while we weren't entirely on the
same wavelength we could appreciate the other's point of view. It
opened my eyes because, until then, I had always thought Graeme to

be rather aloof. Getting to know him over those few days I realised he wasn't like that at all.

I also found that we had a better understanding on the field and at training than we had had before. All the discussions we had helped in making that so. You don't always have to agree. You just have to realise that there are different views on the game – and you can learn from each other.

Graeme, naturally enough, wanted a simple passing game all the time – the Liverpool way. But his problem was that he had played most of his football at Anfield and there they had more than their share of quality footballers. What Graeme had to accept was that life cannot always be that way. I thought there was more to the game than just the Liverpool style but the talks helped both of us. I don't think you could say that we ever disliked each other, but it was just as I said, the great divide was there and we never spent very long in each other's company until then. That time spent up in Queretaro was a bonus for us. We sorted a lot of things out and my only regret is that it hadn't happened sooner.

Under the present régime maybe that would have been the case. The last few times I've been with Scotland I have had different room-mates. I've been with Murdo Macleod and Steve Nicol, so you have the opportunity to get to know players that little bit better. I'm sure that's why Andy arranges it the way he does. He also brings along young players so that when they do get promotion to the full international side they won't arrive in the camp as total strangers, as lads who are maybe a little bit out of their depth. He includes players from the youth team and from the Under-21 side and I think it is a great idea. When we were in San Marino, for instance, young Stephen Wright from Aberdeen was there, as was Alex Rae from Millwall. Andy's system allows them be broken in gradually, so that instead of being over-awed – and that can happen – they can settle in without any trouble when they get their own first full cap. Rather than be starry-eyed over some player they may have hero-worshipped, they have already met the lads when there is no pressure on them. I'm sure this idea will help the young lads in the future.

Being on the other side now – an Anglo – I don't know all the players. But I try to make sure that I get to know them. I'll find out the names of the youngsters and, if I can, I'll sit and have a cup of tea with them and chat about things. I like to think it makes them feel better, maybe more at ease, and, anyhow, it's only common courtesy. The last few times I have been with the Scotland squad I have seen no signs of the divide which had lasted for so long. I think perhaps Andy has healed the rift.

He has gained in stature since taking over the job in the aftermath of the Mexico World Cup in 1986. I mean we all knew how highly rated he was around the world as a coach. He had a higher profile with FIFA for a long time before he was recognised here at home in Scotland. While people may have been surprised when he was handed the job, I don't think he has suffered any by not having the background as a club manager that almost all his predecessors had.

After all, a manager at international level only has the players, in normal circumstances, for a few days at a time. In Andy's words he gets 'a loan' of us. There is not much you can do in that time and man-management, as used by club bosses, doesn't have the same impact at that level. A club manager has your entire future in his hands, the club pays your wages week after week and you cannot exist without playing for your own club side. Because of that you MUST perform for them whenever the demands are made. Those feelings are not around with the national team. You motivate yourself, if you like, and the manager has other things to do. Andy does these well – as professionally as anyone I know.

His administration is first class. The organisation at the training sessions is now worked out to the last possible detail. You don't arrive at a training ground and hang about in the rain while some of the training staff lay out a few cones. Someone has been sent ahead of the main group to have all that prepared for your arrival. Also, you know what training you are going to get, how long it will take and, more or less, what you will be asked to do. Everything is meticulously planned.

He also changes the team hotels around so that players don't get bored with the familiarity of the surroundings. It used to always be either Troon or Turnberry but now we move to different HQs around the country. It can be Gleneagles or Troon or Loch Lomond. It's something else I welcome, because hanging around hotels can be a killer and at least if you have fresh surroundings it helps ease the pain.

His preparations for the actual game itself are excellent, too. He has dossiers on the opposing teams, and these tell you everything you need to know about the team pattern, about the individual players and about the strengths and the weaknesses of the country you have to face. Just going out to play your normal game is no longer enough today, especially at international level. You can't do that. You need information. The more you can get then the better you are going to be able to cope with the demands the games throw up.

There is also more attention paid to what the players are doing in their leisure time. This is always a problem. You arrive after playing in club games, nursing little knocks or more serious injuries, and with the heavy schedule of games we all face, hard training sessions are not always on. So a lot of time is spent relaxing around the hotel.

It used to be that you were left to your own devices. You could walk into the hotel and the lads would be sitting around the lounge drinking maybe their eighteenth cup of tea. That's about all you did then – drink tea! Some of the lads would be racing off to the bookies, others would be watching the horses on the telly or else talking about the game coming up the next Saturday. Or maybe you would be doing something really adventurous – like playing snooker.

Now all of that has changed. Andy has team meetings and talk-ins scheduled and while you have time to yourself you don't find that you have so much that it hangs heavy. He prevents boredom setting in and that is a great thing.

I admit that I was surprised when he was appointed. I think he would admit that he was surprised himself. The old 'Andy who?' comments were flying around but he just got on with the job the way he saw it and while practical experience in the sense of day-to-day involvement with players was not his strong point he has handled the whole situation superbly well. He had been in charge of the Under-18 teams and the Under-21 teams but that was never going to be the same as handling a group of cynical old professionals in the senior side. Yet he has done that and done it impressively. There were suggestions that he would fall down on that part of the job – well, if he has, then I have not been aware of it. Maybe some of the older players found it difficult to accept someone who had no club pedigree as a team boss, but I saw no signs of that. My own view was that if any player was not prepared to accept the new international team manager then he was quite simply a bad professional.

All the players I have spoken to about Andy have been happy at the way he has handled the position. I have pointed out already that the international job is a whole lot different from the club job, so experience at that level might not have been all that important as far as Andy was concerned. Missing out on being a club manager might not have been the handicap it seemed when he was first named. If anything, I think in those early days he was the victim of prejudice in some ways because he was different. He was not in the same mould as the managers who had gone before him. He was, if you like, a theorist. Rated by FIFA, respected in the far-flung football outposts of the world for his coaching know-how, but without the club successes that others had had.

I don't think that matters. All that really counts is his knowledge of the game and his ability to get the best out of the players he has available for selection. If you look at his results over two European Championship campaigns and one World Cup qualifying group, as well as the Italy Finals, you can see that his record matches anyone's.

Maybe more than anything, though, we have to thank him for breaking down the barriers between the home Scots and the Anglos. He has not made it obvious but he has worked away quietly at doing that and in my recent experience he has been successful.

That's maybe as important a contribution to Scotland's cause as any other.

Requiem for a Giant

IN THE GAME OF FOOTBALL, WE ALL TEND TO TALK
about tragedy a lot. We have own goals referred to as "tragic", the
same with mistakes which cost goals or missed scoring chances which
affect a match result. It is only occasionally that you come face to
face with the real thing. Players have had to do that at Ibrox when
the disaster took place there, and at Heysel and Bradford and
Hillsborough when fans died in terrible accidents.

For me the worst moment I have had to handle in my football career
came on a September night in Cardiff in 1985 when Scotland drew
1-1 with Wales but when the result did not matter one little bit. For
that was the night Jock Stein died, a night which will stay with me and
with all the rest of the players who were there for as long as we live.

No one ever expects something like that to happen. No one ever
dreamt that the Scotland manager would die in the dug-out in that
way. No one of my generation could grasp the fact that Jock Stein,
the giant who had dominated the game for so long in Scotland, would
suddenly not be among us. Even now it is hard to accept that the Big
Man is not around. He had given me my first cap back in 1980
during the British International Championships when I played in
Belfast against Northern Ireland. He had stuck by me and some
others despite some bad results – we lost to the Irish 1-0 in my
debut – and when the World Cup qualifying matches arrived I was
still in the side and scored the only goal of the opening tie in Sweden.
It was a goal which helped carry us all the way to Spain and the
finals. Again, it was Big Jock who took me to the finals for the first
time and my Scotland career had run almost parallel with his own
because he had taken over the job late in 1978 when Ally Macleod
resigned after the problems of Argentina.

Eighteen months – and only a handful of games – later I was in his
international set-up. Maybe that's why his death hit me so hard that

night. Maybe, too, it was because I had been ready to fall out with him shortly before he was struck down by the heart attack.

I had been substituted in the second half and I had not been too happy about that. I was sitting on the bench and I suppose I was growling a little bit. He knew that I was not all that happy about being taken off. You never do like to come off and when it is a vital World Cup tie then there is no way you want to leave the field. I didn't say anything to him directly but, while I was moaning away in the dug-out, he suddenly collapsed. I saw him tangle with a photographer on the touch-line right in front of the Scotland bench and then down he went. But none of us realised how serious the collapse was.

With hindsight, you do remember little things that suggested that the Big Man was not one hundred per cent. At the time, though, everything seemed fine apart from the usual tension which does surround these occasions. The way Big Jock used to rid himself of tension was by being continually on the prowl, always chirping at someone, making comments about my height, for example, or kidding another player about a chance he might have missed for his club the previous weekend. That time he was just sitting in the foyer and he was sweating at lunchtime. That was not like him . . . but we didn't give it too much attention.

There are different ways of showing tension. All of us realised that Big Jock was getting older, but nothing more than that – we didn't think he was serously ill. We just put it down to the pressures that managers live with and which he had lived with down through the years. He looked out of sorts, but Alex Ferguson used to show tension in different ways too. You used to hear that dry cough of Fergie's and I mean you could hear it a mile off. You knew that he was worrying over the game which was coming up. I'm sure other managers have little tell-tale signs of their own . . . so, while you recognise they are not themselves, you don't think any more of it. To even imagine that it could cost them their lives is just beyond belief . . . or it was until that night in Cardiff.

I can remember him telling me at half-time that I would be coming off in the second half, allowing Davie Cooper to go on. That was how he wanted to play it and I was ready to argue a little bit when Fergie, who was assistant manager at the time, said to me: "Leave it alone. He's not well. Just leave it." And so I did but none of us thought he was seriously ill. That didn't cross our minds. Even when he did

Jock Stein: the night he died was the worst in my life

collapse on the track we didn't have any idea how bad it was or how tragic it would become.

We were in the dressing-room before we knew what had happened. We were in there sitting around when Fergie told us that Jock had had a heart attack. We all sat there looking at each other and not saying anything. No one was talking about the game. No one was talking about the result. No one was talking about the play-off against Australia we still had to face. No one was talking about Mexico and the World Cup finals the following summer. No one was talking about Big Jock either. It was as if we were afraid to say anything at all.

We were all sitting around in silence wondering what was happening in the little ambulance room next door where Big Jock was getting treatment. Someone came in and said he was fine, that there was some improvement. Someone else came in and said he was worsening and we didn't know what to believe. Then, finally, Alex Ferguson went out. When he returned to the dressing-room he told us that the Big Man had died. It was awful. That is the emptiest I've ever felt. I got dressed and went out through the deserted stand and into the car park past little knots of fans from the Tartan Army who, like myself, were trying to understand how such a thing could have happened. Some of the fans were weeping. Others were standing in a kind of silent tribute. I got into my car and drove back to Manchester and it was the lousiest drive of my life. Something had disappeared from football that night, something which was irreplaceable. You just thought that Jock Stein would go on and on forever. I remembered him as a manager when I was still a kid, still a schoolboy, just a supporter, and he was the most successful manager Scotland had ever seen. Death could hit other people but surely not him. And surely not in such a cruel way.

He had seen everything and he had done everything and now he was dead at a game and we would not be able to turn to him for advice when we were with the Scotland squad in the future. He was the father figure of Scottish soccer. He had won nine Scottish Championships in a row, won the European Cup – the first British manager to do so – won countless other Cups and then guided us to two World Cup finals. He was unique and now he was gone and it was difficult to believe.

Is anything worth that kind of sacrifice? I don't think so and I believe that a lot of people came to realise that on the night Big Jock died.

As players, we knew that going to Mexico suddenly didn't matter nearly as much as it had a few hours earlier. The fans felt the same. There was one man who appeared on the telly and he summed it up for all of us. He said simply: "We would rather have lost the game and still had the Big Man."

It was a terrible loss. He was the kind of manager who looked after his players. He was always very protective of us all. Everyone was in awe of him – players, other managers, pressmen and TV people . . . everyone you met. He was a very wise man. He was certainly a man I would not have liked to take on in a card school. He knew all that was going on. Players couldn't kid him for a moment and very few of us ever tried to. He didn't rant and rave if you did something he didn't like, if you stepped out of line as far as discipline was concerned, for example. He didn't have to do that. You knew, you just knew that he was not happy. And you knew not to step out of line again.

He had tremendous presence and I doubt if any one will ever match his achievements as a manager.

Big Ron's Soccer Academy

RON ATKINSON IS ONE OF THE MOST MISUNDERSTOOD men in football. He has always been a manager who attracts strong opinions. There are no half measures. People either like him or they cannot stand him. The division of opinion runs through all levels of the game – among supporters, media men, players and fellow managers. And you can count me as one of those who like the big man and appreciate what he has tried to do throughout his managerial career.

As far as I'm concerned there has never been another manager like him. Big Ron is a one-off and he has become a very good friend to me. Yet our first meetings did not suggest to me that this friendship would blossom.

First of all, I thought that I was going to have a problem with him on the day I arrived at Old Trafford to sign for Manchester United. As I explain elsewhere in the book, the deal had been initially agreed with the United Chairman, Martin Edwards, while Ron was on holiday in Israel. He came on the scene when I went to Old Trafford for the formal signing and the inevitable Press Conference. So we were both there and when we were left on our own he decided to have a chat with me about his plans for the team in the new season – and the role he expected me to fill in the side. He asked me a few things and I felt that the talk was going well when he suddenly hit me with the clincher. He asked me where I preferred to play in the midfield and I told him that I liked operating in the middle of that area. He looked at me for a moment and then said that that was not at all what he had in mind for me. He had a different role entirely which he wanted me to take over.

His idea was that I would play wide on the right and take over the role that Steve Coppell had held down for United. Nice one, I thought, this is just where I don't want to play. I had spent several seasons having rows with Alex Ferguson about this kind of role. It was not where I enjoyed playing but it was too late for any arguments. This was Manchester United and the start of a new career and all I wanted to do was get off on the right foot and see if I could get myself established at Old Trafford.

But this was not what I would have chosen for myself. No way. The times that Aberdeen had used me in that way, that wide position on the right, had not been the happiest of times for me. I always felt better when Alex used three men in the midfield rather than the two men which Ron was going to use, with two wide players ready to come into deep positions when the team lost possession. Most of the time at Pittodrie I had responsibilities for the right-hand side of the midfield while Peter Weir patrolled the left flank. But I was not tied down to the role the way Big Ron seemed to want when the season started. Anyway, there was no way that I was going to rock the boat by voicing my doubts and objections. I had gone through enough troubled times to get there without causing bother on my first day. Still, there is no denying that I felt some shivers of apprehension over being told that I would be filling a role in the team which I simply did not enjoy. Yet, as things unfolded and I grew to know Ron better, I found out that playing in any team where he was boss was a joy. He helped give me some of my most enjoyable moments in football.

He was a whole lot different from Alex Ferguson in his approach to the job but they had one thing in common – a deep passion for the game. Now, I know that a lot of you won't be ready to believe that about Ron. All people can see sometimes are the flash suits and the jewellery and the larger-than-life presence that Big Ron has. I don't see anything wrong with the fact that he dresses well. After all, anyone who is a success in his chosen profession should dress well. That is expected. Why should football managers by any different? Yet Ron gets stick for that. It's unfair and it leads to a serious misjudgment of the man. There is far more to Ron Atkinson than the "Flash Harry" tag that is hung around his neck by people who simply don't know him and by others who haven't taken the time to get to know him properly. OK, on the surface there is no one you could meet who is less like Alex Ferguson than Big Ron and yet they share this love for the game even though they may display it in different ways. When you meet Ron away from the public gaze, all he wants to do is talk football – that's the same as Alex. Exactly the same. Anything to do with the game is bread and butter to him. Quiz

*The Tartan Army who greeted me at Old Trafford – Gordon McQueen, Arthur
Graham, yours truly, Arthur Albiston, Graeme Hogg and Alan Brazil, with
Ron Atkinson there as an honorary member*

questions, any piece of trivia, gossip from international matches and
get-togethers, talk about other players, what's happening at other
clubs, tactics you have come up against. Any and all of that is what
makes Big Ron happy. Just as long as you are talking football and
football people then he is at his best and his most relaxed and entertaining. Alex Ferguson is the same.

Yet, in the methods they use to run a club, they are as different as
night and day. I recognised that from the very first day of training at
The Cliff, United's training ground. And it was a surprise to me . . .

It was far, far different from any of the training sessions I was
used to having at Pittodrie with Alex Ferguson and Archie Knox.
Remember, this was the first day's training after the summer break
and traditionally it's the day when managers and coaches try to find
out how high you have kept your fitness levels in the weeks away.
Basically, it is a hard day, a tough day, one where you know you
are going to be made to sweat. The only thing is that no one seemed
to have told Ron that. There he was with this marvellous suntan
from his holiday in Israel, wearing only shorts. He told us to start a

seven-a-side game. I couldn't believe it . . . Then he wandered off base. We started playing and he kept walking until he found a nice spot in the sun to lie down on. We were left to get on with the game. I think the only real instruction came when he looked at the three new signings – myself, Jesper Olsen and Alan Brazil – and commented: "Right, on you go and let's see what I've spent all my money on this summer." I thought, this is just like Alex and Archie! They would have been putting us through the mill, hammering us and shouting at us and not giving anyone a moment's rest. By comparison, that first day at The Cliff was like a day at Butlin's!

There were other contrasts, too, from the style of management I was accustomed to. Fergie used fear as a motivator. He scared people – although I don't know if he is the same now. He may have mellowed a little. But at the time I'm talking about he could be a frightening character. He could put the fear of death into players just to get them to play the way he wanted them to play. It was almost a test of character when he had a go at you. He wanted to know if you had enough bottle to stand up to him – and that would prove that you had the same bottle to help you succeed on the park. He could be scathing and he could hurt you because at times he would become personal if he thought that would help him get what he wanted from you. He would do it to wind people up, make verbal assaults on players at half-time, and then, when he left the dressing-room, would wink at someone like myself who had not been the target. Meanwhile some poor player would be left sitting a shattered wreck.

Yet for all of this Fergie is likeable and he cares about players. I have spoken to Mark McGhee about this and we agree that you could never learn to love Alex but neither would you dislike him. You couldn't fall in love with him because of his abrasive management style but he felt that he needed that to succeed. Results may have proved him right.

Ron, on the other hand, would try to coax better performances from his players. It was so different from Alex but it could be just as effective. He would wheedle better displays out of players. Then if, that didn't work, he would be as ruthless as Alex because if a player did not respond to his style of man-management and simply wasn't doing it for him or for the team, he would be sold. Ron would just get rid of anyone like that. He didn't hesitate either. One day the lad would be there, the next he would be on his bike and someone else

A tussle with an old team-mate. Brian McClair and myself are involved in this on-the-ground tangle in a match against my old club Manchester United

would be drafted in. Of course, that was a luxury that Alex didn't have. Ron could move into the transfer market and spend huge amounts of money to get the men he wanted and he did just that. The team was like a toy to Ron, something which he created to give himself pleasure as well as bring United the success the club and the huge support demanded.

Ron likes his teams to follow his own flamboyant approach to life. He wanted entertaining teams. He wanted players who were superb individualists. He wanted to see United attacking in every game. Attack, attack, attack – he didn't ask for anything else from us. At that time it suited me down to the ground. It was exhilarating to play in that kind of team where everyone was bubbling, where the football was flowing and where you were encouraged to express yourself and enjoy yourself out on the field. Now I realise that all the nice little flicks, all the cheeky back-heels and all the nutmegs count for nothing if you are not winning. You have to win games if you are to be truly successful. Yet, I doubt if Ron ever looks at things that way. His teams have always been entertaining and attractive. That has been his trademark and he won't change now. The thing is that Ron enjoys the nice little touches that supporters love to see but which don't always bring success. And yet it's hard to argue against his philosophy because he has had success. He had it with United – apart from failing to win the First Division Championship – and he had it again last season when Sheffield Wednesday won the League Cup at Wembley. His record as a manager is superb and it's good to see someone get success with a policy which puts entertainment very high on any list of soccer priorities.

Ron was an unbelievable man. He was good for me in those years we had together at Old Trafford. Away from the limelight he could be hurt by the criticism his high-profile image brought him. Somehow the fans didn't totally accept him even though his record was tremendous. He was always being criticised and more often than not the abuse he took was unfair.

He was in the top four in the First Division just about every season he was in charge at Old Trafford. He won the FA Cup twice and he took the team to a semi-final spot in the European Cup Winners' Cup. As well as that, he fashioned teams that United fans should have been able to identify with. These were teams playing good football and the type of football that had always been a part of the United tradition. I saw more pure football played at Old Trafford in my time there than I saw in the rest of my career. There were some superb games played by Ron Atkinson's teams, but he failed because he did not bring the title back to Manchester. That is the prize they want more than any other, more even than the European trophy Alex Ferguson won for them last season in Rotterdam.

We had that marvellous run of ten wins on the trot when it looked as if the title was going to be won at last and then it all fell apart because of injuries. I'll go into that in detail later in this chapter.

Anyhow, when we did not get the title that season I think that Ron lost heart. He believed that that was the best team he had been able to put together at Old Trafford. It played the football he wanted. We were also winning games with style. It should all have been perfect and for a spell at the start of that season it was. We had won the Cup the previous season, in May 1985. Then we started off superbly again. But, at the end of that season, Ron looked as if he had had the heart knocked out of him. It was a difficult time for him

On the receiving end this time as young Lee Sharpe tries to get to grips with me in a clash with the Old Trafford team

because the disappointment hit him hard – much harder than I had expected. Probably because the title had looked to be in his grasp and the prize that the club wants so desperately was torn from him.

When the next season loomed you could see that it was going to be hard for him. In some ways the writing was on the wall but the players all wanted him to stay on as manager. I went to see him in the summer and told him that. I knocked on the manager's door, went in to see him and asked him to stick it out, to have another go for the title. He did try but it was not the same. Maybe it was never going to be the same. As well as Ron hurting from the League slump the previous season, the players were suffering a hangover from our collapse in the title race. There were still good players at the club – and I told Ron that when I talked to him – but we never did recapture that heady early-season form which had swept us to such an early title lead a year earlier. It was a marvellous spell while it lasted, but it didn't last long enough – not for the club, not for the players and certainly not for Ron, who was sacked a few months into the season.

It was harsh and it must have been difficult for Ron to accept but, deep down, he must have known, as all United's managers have known since Sir Matt Busby, that if you cannot deliver the Championship flag then your neck is on the line. It now seemed to be an apt time for a change because, despite my message of hope in the summer when the season began, Ron now seemed unable to lift the players. All the coaxing in the world was not working for him. Some of us obviously thought that our hopes of a title medal had now disappeared and we were playing as if we did not believe that our glorious run of form could ever be repeated. So it was time for a change and Alex Ferguson stepped back into my life. He was, without doubt, the right man for the job. He had the stature and he had the winning credentials which United were looking for. If anyone can win them the title then I'm sure Alex Ferguson is that man.

Everything about Old Trafford was so different from what I had known in Aberdeen . . . and I'm not just talking about Big Ron's approach to the game. The whole set-up was geared to keeping players happy. I mean, all you have to do at Old Trafford is play football – everything else is done for you. Every aspect of your life and your family's life is looked after for you. You don't have to worry about a thing. Their motto seems to be "a player without a worry is a better player". They arranged a doctor and a dentist and a lawyer for you. They looked after your insurances and they even helped arrange family holidays for you. Nothing was too much for them. If you were doing a job for the club on the field, then they provided the very best for you off the field. We stayed in the best hotels when we were playing away from home. We ate in the best restaurants and everything about the club was first class. I'm not trying to run down Aberdeen any, but United were on a different financial footing from the Pittodrie club and it showed in all kinds of ways.

I found it easy to settle in at Old Trafford because there was the usual Scottish contingent there. Gordon McQueen looked after me when I first arrived. Then there was Arthur Albiston – I had played with him in schools' football back in Edinburgh. Arthur Graham, the former Aberdeen player, was there too – he was very good to me even though it looked very much as if I was there to take over the role he had been playing in the team. Ron had been using him in that wide-on-the-right role which had been held down by Steve Coppell for so many seasons at Old Trafford. Arthur had been a kind of a stop-gap in that position and now here I was taking over. It could have been a difficult situation but he made it easy for me.

The only real success I knew at United was winning the FA Cup in my first full season with the club. That was marvellous, though the opening to the following season when I helped in that long unbeaten run also brought me a lot of pleasure. But winning the Cup in my first season in English soccer was superb for me. Especially as it seemed to be a continuation of the glory run I had enjoyed with Aberdeen before making the move south. My last years at Pittodrie had brought me three Scottish Cup medals in a row, with victories at Hampden over Rangers, twice, and Celtic. It seemed a good omen that a Wembley victory should follow on immediately after that Scottish hat-trick. I had gone a helluva long time without losing a Cup tie. That was a four-year spell, remember, and I think it may be some kind of a record.

We started off, I remember, with a home tie against Bournemouth. Back in Scotland with Aberdeen, that kind of tie would have been looked on as a walk-over. But that was not the attitude at Old Trafford. Far from it! The previous season United had been drawn against the same team in the first round and they had lost 2-0. That was when they were starting off to defend the trophy they had won the season before after beating Brighton in a replayed final. To be asked to play Bournemouth again a year later sent jitters running through the whole place. I could not understand it – but I do now and did by the time I became used to the Cup games in England. They are different.

I know there are always the odd shock results in Scotland. Rangers lost to Berwick. Then the Ibrox men lost to Hamilton a few years ago in a first-round match at Ibrox. But these shocks are much more likely to happen down south. The FA Cup records are littered with surprises. Just a year earlier United had become one of those statistics and the fear was there that history would repeat itself.

As it happened, it didn't. We won the game comfortably by 3-0. I scored the first goal in twenty minutes and that helped settle us down. In fact, we were cruising after that. We didn't have a problem in the game, but scoring early had helped and we remained on the road to Wembley and the final.

It was Blackburn Rovers in the next round, away from home, and it was a brick-hard playing surface for this Friday-night game, live on television. This time I knew how the lads had felt about the first match – because I was nervous. This was the kind of fixture where shocks easily occur. A bad ground, a Second Division team fired up at the arrival of Manchester United and a huge television audience ready to back the underdogs. It was a classic situation for a giant-killing act and I suppose we all recognised the potential for disaster that lurked. However, my Cup luck was still potent and I scored the first goal again, fastening on to a short pass back and then chipping the ball over the 'keeper. I can still recall that the goalie seemed sure that I was going to try to carry the ball round him and I took him by surprise with the chip. I surprised myself as well . . . but in it went. Paul McGrath added another and it was all over. When we beat West Ham next time out I began to feel that this was going to be another Cup success for yours truly. You can get those feelings some-times – a kind of sixth sense which tells you that this is a tournament where you can't go wrong, and this was one of them.

My Hampden hat-trick seemed to be carried over to this fresh career and, while we were not able to make an impact on the League, this was the Cup. Everyone knows that it is not always the best team in the country which takes the title – it is the team which can carry luck and ally that to ability on certain days. We were not consistent enough for a Championship-winning team, but we had superb players and we had the flair which Big Ron insisted on. There was a natural excitement about our play, an exuberance but also a resilience which did suggest that, like Aberdeen, we had a Cup win in front of us.

It's a good feeling to have, something which can sustain you through a season when other things may be going wrong. We began to get that lift. The solid way we had marched past Bournemouth and Blackburn in tricky ties and then been able to dispose of West Ham handed all of us a boost in confidence for the even more testing games which lay ahead of us.

That game against the Hammers still gives me a laugh when I think back to it – though the incident was not funny at the time. The match was at Old Trafford and I was pulled down in the penalty-box by one of their defenders. When I got up, there was this tremendous hush around the ground. Fifty thousand people seemed to be holding their breath, waiting to see if I was going to take the kick myself. You see, I had been going through a terrible time and I'd had a sequence of penalties which was something like four misses out of five. This time it was too much for me even to consider. I just got up, turned round and walked away out of the box. There was this huge collective sigh of relief which just seemed to sweep round the whole of the stadium. It was like fifty thousand of our fans saying, "Oh, thank God for that." Norman Whiteside stepped up and tucked the kick away and another win was chalked up. Wembley came that little bit closer.

But before getting there we had Liverpool to face – Liverpool, the team who seemed able to win the prize we wanted almost at will. This was one year they were going to miss out – but they had taken the title in the three previous seasons. We used to think that all we wanted to do was win it once – just once to end the jinx which had been hanging over the club for so long. Anyhow, Liverpool had their own hoodoo and that was in the FA Cup. So we felt that we were going to have the edge over them when it came to the semi-final at Goodison. We did well in that game, really well, and we were twice in the lead. Mark Hughes scored the first one and Frank Stapleton got the second. We were in front as the game moved into injury time. There we were leading 2-1 and I could see the twin towers at the end of Wembley Way in my mind's eye when the ball broke to Kenny Dalglish and I was left with the job of tackling him. Not the easiest task in the world, I must say, but yet there was no excuse for the pathetic challenge I did make. Well, there was, actually. Instead of just going into the tackle, I tried to out-think Kenny. Not the

I'm not going down this time as I squeeze past this despairing tackle from an unidentified Manchester United defender

brightest thing to do. I lost. He pushed the ball through my legs and went away from me. Then he crossed. Paul Walsh scored. The game was level and everyone was looking at me. It was all down to me. It was a body blow for us to suffer when victory was so close. But the lads were good – they didn't say too much.

Then we had to go to Maine Road for the replay which was a classic match. Both of them were classics, I suppose, but that first one is spoiled for me a little bit by the memory of the awful tackle I tried to make. Most people thought we had blown it because we had played so well in that first game and then allowed them to come back twice – first with a wonderful goal from Ronnie Whelan and then with the equaliser. When you give Liverpool second chances then they usually take them. That was what everyone was telling us. They scored first through John Wark and we went in at half-time a goal down and, no doubt, being written off by everyone in the country. But somehow we managed to come back at them in that second half. Bryan Robson scored our first and then I can remember beating Alan Hansen and pushing the ball through for Mark Hughes to grab the winner. It was a famous victory for us. My Cup run kept rolling along . . .

Now it was the final and another Mersey team stood between us and success. Everton had taken the title – just to keep it in the city – and they had also won the European Cup Winners' Cup against Rapid Vienna that season. We stood between them and a magnificent treble. But we were determined to do it. They were on a golden run for the club under their manager Howard Kendall. They had won the Cup the previous season and they were a terrific side. Up front were two of my Scotland mates, Graeme Sharp and Andy Gray. At that time they were the most lethal front pairing in English football! Neville Southall was in goal, Gary Stevens and Trevor Steven were in the side and they had truly emerged from the shadow of their great Anfield rivals to make their own reputation at home and in Europe. It was an incredible accomplishment for a club which had had to live for so many years as the underdog in the same city as the team which dominated English and European football. It said a lot about Everton's character as well as their ability that they had broken clear of that.

All of us knew that this was going to be as difficult a game as the two semi-finals had been and we prepared for that. The Cup final was all that was left for us in the season and I gathered my Cup run around me as if it was a talisman which would bring me another medal in my first season in the First Division.

It was to be a tremendous experience for me whatever happened because by this time I had realised that without doubt the FA Cup final stands second only to the World Cup final in terms of prestige and a sense of occasion. It's the biggest in the world, the best at club level. I don't know anything that compares to it.

It's a shame when I think back to the Scottish Cup finals I played in. I won a medal three years in succession with Aberdeen and yet it was just like going into the old routine every May. Down to the Excelsior Hotel at Glasgow Airport on the Friday afternoon, have a meal, off to bed, then up in the morning for a little loosening up. Pick up your comps for the match and then off to Hampden. It should be done a bit better. I don't know how you could do it but, at the moment, it remains very much the poor relation to the English event. I'm not suggesting that in terms of the games and how they are played – quite often the Scottish final throws up the more exciting match – but I'm talking about what goes on round about the event. The FA Cup final is one of the major sporting events in the world, not just a football occasion but a true sporting occasion which ranks with the Derby or the British Open or the Wimbledon final as something to be seen. It is also something you should be seen at. The glamour and the showbiz swamp anything that poor old Hampden can offer.

I mean, last season I was at home and watching the two finals, switching channels back and forward to get a look at both the Scottish and English games. The match between Dundee United and Motherwell had all the excitement and all the drama but I was always lured back to Wembley because of the way the game was presented and because the atmosphere has a special kind of magic about it, no matter how good or bad the finals are.

The build up as far as the media is concerned is much more intense down south. Television, for example, seems to kick off twenty-four hours ahead of the match. You see shots of the players at their hotels the day before the match once they have moved into their favourite pre-final headquarters. On the morning of the game you are with the players again. The cameras are on the team buses as they head for the stadium and they are with the fans hours before kick-off to sustain the build in excitement. Scotland just doesn't do it that way. The FA Cup final is also more of a family affair than the final in Scotland. Up at home it's still a case of the lads coming out of the pub and off to the game at half-past two or so. And if they're not going then they'll stay in the pub and watch it there. In the south the family go and the family watch. TOGETHER. A whole load of showbiz is also injected into the FA final – all kinds of celebrities are paraded in front of the cameras, either TV stars or pop stars or radio stars or disc jockeys, and all of them have their favourite team. They give their verdicts and it's all part of a fun day before the real business commences. The final belongs to the whole nation. In Scotland it's still men only and, to a large extent still, it only involves the supporters of the two teams competing in the final on that day. It just isn't the same and yet it could be if people worked a little harder on the presentation side.

I must say, I thoroughly relished the whole thing. I don't know how I would have been if I was still a youngster going into a game like that. But I wasn't. I had a few Hampden appearances under my belt and, while the publicity is nothing like as intense, it remains a national final. A few years earlier, while with Aberdeen, I had decided to enjoy the finals more. When you start off winning your first medal, you find youself dancing round the pitch at the end with a silly hat or scarf on and then when you try to remember the game you find that you can't. I was determined now to try to enjoy the whole thing more and store away some of the memories. I think it was Gothenburg and the European Cup Winners' final when Aberdeen beat Real Madrid to take the trophy that I began my new approach to Cup finals. I just wanted to take it all in. You can enjoy it all a whole lot more if you take a look at the faces of the fans, if you look at the kids and all the people who have paid a lot of money to come to see you and you try to share their joy. Instead of being self-indulgent and doing your wee dance on the pitch, it's better when you try to involve yourself with the emotions that the fans feel. I have tried that and it has been good for me. It has helped make these occasions that bit more memorable.

It was that way with Wembley. It started well. Fergie gave me a phone in the morning to wish me good luck and to tell me he would be at the game because that was one year Aberdeen did not reach the Scottish final. I must have stolen their luck and taken it with me to Old Trafford! Still, Fergie forgave me that, wished me well and then turned up at the reception at night to congratulate me on winning an FA Cup medal. We were at the Royal Lancaster. Fergie came in and big Gary Bailey, our goalkeeper, thought he was my Dad. "Hello,

Mr Strachan," he said and Fergie was not amused. Still, he stayed on and we had a good night. It was as if we had never had our differences. I appreciated the fact that he had gone out of his way to phone and then to come to the party as well. It was very ironic that a year and a half later he ended up as manager of the club.

Everton were at their best then. They were really buzzing and they had all these international players I've mentioned. We knew this was a hard one but we also knew it would be a great football match. I like to think it was. Big Ron simply preached his usual philosophy about the game and sent us out on to Wembley to play the kind of football he believed in and the kind of football which is always associated with the United tradition. And we won. The turning point of the game, I think, was the ordering off of Kevin Moran for an innocuous tackle. He should never have gone. It was a bad decision by the referee. Kevin had made a tackle on Peter Reid, the Everton midfield player, and Peter had gone down. Suddenly the referee was ordering poor Kevin off. It was the ref's last game – I mean, his last ever game before retiring – and the FA had given him the final as a long-service award. He decided to make the headlines, and it could have ruined the game but instead the match caught fire because all of us were so upset at what had happened.

It was late in the game, maybe quarter of an hour from the end. Being Wembley and being the usual warm day that Cup finals invariably produce, we were all tiring. The advantage should have moved in Everton's direction but it didn't happen exactly that way. We held out until the end and then in extra time everyone in the side took on the extra responsibility and worked that little bit harder. We deserved to win the game in the end. No one could argue, especially with the quality of the winner – big Norman Whiteside scored as good a goal as you have ever seen at Wembley. I'll never forget it. I had raised my last gallop to a run from the middle of the field when he took possession. I went past him in an overlap and I was shouting for the ball and looking for the pass to come when Norman turned inside with it. I though he was just heading into trouble. We had no one in their box who could help him. If it had been a game of snooker then Norman was snookered. In fact, that is exactly the situation he found himself in and so he chalked the toe of his boot and shot. He curled this magnificent drive past Neville Southall to give us victory. I'll never forget that.

It was the kind of goal which Big Ron loved to see. As far as he was

I must have done something right here! The defender is down this time and I'm still in possession

concerned, that was the only way you should win trophies. Not by efficiency, but by brilliance. I used to think that Ron would be quite happy if we lost a game 6-4 as long as he could look back and say that we had scored the best goal of the game. That one of Norman's was made for Ron. Made in heaven. It was not out of any coaching manual, it was a superb strike from a superb player. You can't get better than that, can you?

It meant a lot to Ron, that victory, just as it meant a lot to all of us. The big fella deserved it because in my book he has always been a manager who wants to see the best of football. He stuck to these principles all through his career and I'm glad to say it has brought him success. If there is any criticism it is just that he insists on the purest football even at the expense of results. That can be annoying but it says a lot for the man and his beliefs.

For myself, it was a little bit special because when you go down there the lads always kid you on a bit about winning medals in Scotland. It's always that kind of thing, suggesting that there is no one to beat in Scotland and so the medals don't count as much. They do, of course. But to get that FA medal to add to my collection after just a season with United meant a lot to me. I think it meant that I had gone almost five years without being in a losing FA Cup side, so that was something else I enjoyed on a personal level. But my feelings were mainly for United and their fans. I had been one of the new players bought to help them get success and while the title still eluded the club, at least I had made a contribution in helping them to another Cup win. And we had done it the hard way, taking on the might of Merseyside – teams who were in European finals that season. Liverpool were in that tragic European Cup final when they lost to Juventus at the Heysel disaster and Everton lifted the Cup Winners' Cup. It was something to write home about.

Hey, and it had happened at Wembley in the biggest British game of all. The First Division title apart, I could not have asked for any more. A perfect result in the most perfect setting.

There was a brief European interlude that season, too. We played in the UEFA Cup and that was the last time I played club football in any of the continental competitions. The ban followed and since then I have not been with a team which has qualified.

We were knocked out on penalties by the Hungarian side Videoton in the quater-finals. But it was the third-round clash which brought most excitement – a Battle of Britain against Dundee United. From being on the other side of these Scotland v England games, I knew what we were in for when the draw was announced. I told the lads what to expect. It was going to be tougher than any of the other games because of the amount of national pride which would come into play. Also, United had a tremendous European record under Jim McLean. Just the year before, they had gone to the semi-final of the European Cup and only lost narrowly to Italian champions Roma. This was never going to be an easy game. But, funnily enough, we were given a helping hand by Fergie, though it was totally unintentional. He went on telly to say he fancied United to beat us because they were far fitter than we were and they would run us off the park. That wound the lads up.

We drew 2-2 in the first match at Old Trafford but we had deserved to win the game. I scored with one penalty and missed another that night and Hamish McAlpine was outstanding for them. They played well. We knew the second leg at Tannadice was going to present us with even more problems than we had had on our own home ground. However, we went there, won 3-2 and that result pushed us into the tournament's last eight.

Again, Alex said he thought we would go out and again it had us more than a little bit annoyed. The lads didn't like it and I can remember big Gordon McQueen in Dundee Airport after the game doing one-handed press-ups and saying: "How would Mr Ferguson like to see this? An athlete at work." And there he was doing these press-ups with a lager in his other hand. It was good for the Scots in our side to go up there and get that result. If we'd lost we would have had a lot of stick. They had good players – Paul Sturrock, Dave Narey, Paul Hegarty, Eamon Bannon – and they were at their peak around that time. It was a wonderful result for us. There was no way I wanted to go back up home and lose – especially to United who had been Aberdeen's greatest north-east rivals for so many years. I had never liked losing to them and I didn't want to go down to them again. I don't think I could have handled listening to Jim McLean on the telly after the game if we had lost that one. That would have been too much.

The next season brought the joy of playing in that long winning run as we started after the title . . . and the sadness of blowing it before the end. That sensational sprint start had us so far in front. We should have been able to build on that even when the wheels started to come off . . . but we didn't and that was the one glimpse of the title I had in all my years at Old Trafford.

Still, it was a privilege to play in the team during that spell. We had ten wins on the trot which gave us thirty points and then we went another five games before losing. Funnily enough, it was Howard Wilkinson's Sheffield Wednesday team which defeated us. Even more strange, it was Sheffield Wednesday, again, who ended United's unbeaten run this season. This time they had gone twelve games without losing. Wednesday had the Indian sign on them again. They beat them 3-2 and toppled them from top spot in the First Division. (And guess who took over from them there? Yes, we did – it was a good, good feeling.)

Going back, though, that spell we had happened when all our players peaked at the one time and everyone wanted to play football. Everyone wanted to push the ball around and make passes and entertain. I went out after ten games when I ran into a post at West Brom and that started a series of injuries. I dislocated my shoulder and then, gradually, other players picked up knocks and we didn't have the ability to sustain our challenge. The change in the game was just coming then, all the long-ball stuff, all the pressure play, all the kind of things you expect from the Wimbledons of this world. We could not combat that properly. We found it hard to handle that type of opposition. When the heavier grounds arrived and the injuries mounted, we dropped out of the challenge and finally finished fourth.

Sheffield Wednesday, the team which ended the run, were playing that kind of power game. They were getting the ball very quickly from back to front. They were working on set pieces and using long throw-ins to put defences in trouble. Big Ron's team talk used to last two minutes and we were not prepared for some of the tactical changes that were occurring. Basically, Ron believed that if you had the best players then you would win games. Unhappily, it doesn't always work that way. We found that out for ourselves the hard way and, while we floundered, Liverpool just ground out result after result to take the Championship again.

We used to play well against Liverpool, you know, and I think it was Ron who had the secret of stopping them. He used to make sure that big Alan Hansen did not get time on the ball. He used to tell us to mark Alan as tightly as you would mark any forward. That kept him from setting up their attacks from those deep positions. We also cut down on the space he was allowed to stop him going on those dangerous runs forward. It worked. Alan and Kenny were the main dangers by that time and if you could curb them then you had chances. But I think they were just that bit more resilient than we were. They were used to winning titles – we were not. The pressure got to some of the lads, too. There's no doubt about it, there is a helluva lot of pressure when you are at Old Trafford. There are players who cannot handle that. They come from provincial clubs and are thrust into the spotlight and they crack up.

It was a sad end to what had promised to be the season to remember. That was the best spell of football I was ever involved in. It remains, though, a time of regret because it all fell apart. I went out and others went out and the magic was never recaptured. When Bryan Robson was injured soon after me it was all over. The dreams died and for Ron the party had ended. He never really recovered and that meant that he lost his job the following season. The title jinx claimed another victim.